Ageing Matters

ISSUES
(formerly Issues for the Nineties)

Volume 16

Editor

Craig Donnellan

Independence
Educational Publishers
Cambridge

First published by Independence
PO Box 295
Cambridge CB1 3XP
England

British Library Cataloguing in Publication Data
Ageing Matters – (Issues Series)
I. Donnellan, Craig II. Series
331.3'98

ISBN 1 86168 092 9

Printed in Great Britain
The Burlington Press
Cambridge

Typeset by
Claire Boyd

Cover
The illustration on the front cover is by
Pumpkin House.

CONTENTS

Chapter One: The Older Population

The retired population 1

Our ageing world – the facts 2

The ageing of the world's population 3

Older women 4

UK lifespan 'is heading toward 80' 5

You're never too young to be old 6

A life in the South is 7 years longer 7

Ageing process 8

Population ageing – a public health challenge 9

Life expectancy at birth for both sexes 10

The UN principles for older persons 11

Pensions timebomb 12

Income 13

Chapter Two: Ageism in the Workplace

Age – the issues for today's workplace 15

Age discrimination 16

Age prejudice 'costs Britain £26bn a year' 18

The real cost of ageism 19

Ministers outlaw age limits on jobs 20

Don't snub the golden oldies, bosses urged 21

Broken promises 22

Private lives 23

Chapter Three: Health and Care Issues

Healthy ageing 25

Home truths 26

Town halls 'still plundering the elderly in care' 27

When older people need care . . . 28

Old people's homes 'hide the true cost' 29

The 'invisible' patients 30

Family break-ups 'spell disaster for care of the elderly' 31

Elder abuse 32

Mental illness 34

Understanding and respecting the person with dementia 36

What is Alzheimer's disease? 38

Challenging dementia 39

Living to be 100? It is nearly all in the mind 40

Additional resources 41

Index 42

Web site information 43

Acknowledgements 44

Introduction

Ageing Matters is the sixteenth volume in the series: **Issues**. The aim of this series is to offer up-to-date information about important issues in our world.

Ageing Matters looks at ageing matters, discrimination in the workplace, health and care issues.

The information comes from a wide variety of sources and includes:
Government reports and statistics
Newspaper reports and features
Magazine articles and surveys
Literature from lobby groups
and charitable organisations.

It is hoped that, as you read about the many aspects of the issues explored in this book, you will critically evaluate the information presented. It is important that you decide whether you are being presented with facts or opinions. Does the writer give a biased or an unbiased report? If an opinion is being expressed, do you agree with the writer?

Ageing Matters offers a useful starting-point for those who need convenient access to information about the many issues involved. However, it is only a starting-point. At the back of the book is a list of organisations which you may want to contact for further information.

*****

The retired population

Information from Help the Aged

The number of older people in the UK

The number of older people in the population has increased over the past decades, and is projected to increase in the future.

The ageing population

Despite the increase in the total number of older people, the overall percentage of people over 65 is projected to remain constant for some time at around 15-16% of the total population. The number of people aged between 65 and 79 is actually projected to fall slightly in the next 10 years.

However, the section of the population which is increasing, both in actual size and in relation to the total population, is that of people over 80. The proportion of people in this age group is projected to increase from 1.9% in 1961 to 4.0% in 2001. Thus, even though the proportion of older people (65+) in the population is remaining more or less constant, an increasing number in this group will be very elderly. This could have a significant impact on such issues as the provision of support services in the community.

Pensionable age

In 1994, there were 10.6 million people of pensionable age in the UK (*Regional Trends* 31, 1996, table 15.1). This represents 18.2% of the total population of the UK. The total for just Great Britain, as shown in the 1991 Census, is 10.3 million, 18.7% of the population as a whole. Pensionable age at present is 60 for women and 65 for men. It has been argued that this difference leads to discrimination (against both women and men, in different circumstances). The Government proposes to equalise the state pension age for men and women at 65, although this change is not intended to happen until 2010.

Life expectancy

In 1997, life expectancy at birth in the UK is expected to be 74 years for men and nearly 80 years for women (*Social Trends* 27, 1997, chart 7.1). Life expectancy increases with age: in England, a man aged 60 can expect to life a further 18.7 years to 78.7 and a woman aged 60 a further 22.6 years to 82.6 (*Health and Personal Social Services Statistics* 1998, tables A1 and A2).

Life expectancy in the UK has increased steadily throughout this century. In 1931, life expectancy at birth was 58.4 (men) and 62.4 (women), and in 1961, 67.9 and 73.8 years respectively.

Gender structure

Women's higher life expectancy is demonstrated clearly in the male/female divide in the older population. In 1995, men formed 49% of the population of the UK as a whole, but only 34% of those aged over 75.

Retired households

One-third (32%) of all households in Great Britain are headed by a person aged 60 or over. Moreover, one in six (16%) of all households in Great Britain consist of one person aged 60+ living alone (*General Household Survey* 1996, table 2.2).

What kind of households do older people live in?

The vast majority of people over pensionable age live in private (that is, non-institutional) housing. Only approximately 5% of people in this age group live in a residential or nursing home. Of those living in private housing, more than a third (39%) live on their own. Just under half, 48%, live just with their partner and 13% live with other people such as a son, daughter or siblings (*General Household Survey* 1996, table 8.43).

Over three-quarters of the elderly population therefore live either on their own or just with their partner in private housing. This demonstrates that, contrary to stereotype, most older people live independent lives in the community.

© *Help the Aged*

1

Our ageing world – the facts

Rapidly ageing populations

One of the major achievements of the 20th century has been an increase in life expectancy in almost every country in the world. At the same time fewer children are being born as people become more able to plan their families. These two factors mean that across the world populations are getting older – with a high number of older people and a smaller proportion of younger people. This population change is happening fastest in less-developed countries.

Some countries still have a low life expectancy. This does not mean that there are no older people in these countries. In countries where life expectancy is lower than 65, those who do reach this age have a further life expectancy of some 11 to 14 years. For example, in Bangladesh the life expectancy for women at birth is 54.7 years. Women who reach the age of 65 can expect to live a further 12-13 years.

Some facts about our ageing world

- In 1995 the number of people aged 60 years and over across the world increased by more than 12 million people (over 1 million people a month). Nearly 80% of this increase took place in the developing world.
- It is estimated that by 2030 nearly three-quarters of people aged 60 and over will be living in less-developed countries.
- The speed at which less-developed countries are ageing is much greater than in industrialised nations. For example, it took 115 years for the older population of France to increase from 7 to 17%, but a comparable change will occur in China in just 27 years.
- In Brazil in 1996, the average age of the population was 25 years. In 2025 it is expected to be 35 years. In Guadeloupe in 1996 the average age was 28 – in 2025 it will be 40.

- Some less-developed countries, such as Colombia, Costa Rica, Liberia and Venezuela, are expected to experience an increase of more than 200% in their older populations in the next 25 years.
- Older people, especially in developing countries, often continue to work and support their families. In Zimbabwe, 82% of men and 70% of women over 60 are still economically active. Older people who are not undertaking paid work are often doing work which is not paid, such as childcare, managing the home and agricultural work for their families. This often enables other family members to take on paid work outside the home.

An ageing world is a female world

- Nearly everywhere, women outlive men. At 60 years old there are 99 males to every 100 females. At the age of 80 and over, there are just 69 males to every 100 females.

- Women often outlive their spouses, meaning they are more likely to be living alone in old age. In many countries of Africa and Asia, more than half of all women aged 60 and over are widowed, compared to 10-20% of men. Women are also less likely than men to remarry if their spouse has died.

The oldest old

- In less-developed countries in 1996, almost one-fifth of the older population was aged 75 or over.
- In many countries of the world the oldest old (75 years and over) are the fastest growing portion of the older population.
- More than a quarter of all people aged 75 or older live in just two countries – China and India.

Credit: Most of the information in this page comes from the United States Department of Commerce Economics and Statistics Administration, Bureau of the Census. Further information can be obtained on: http://www.census.gov/ipc/www/
© Helpage International

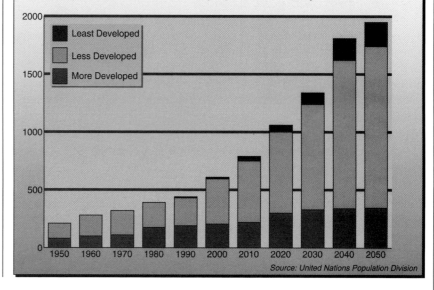

World population aged 60 and over, 1950-2050

Over the past few years, the world's population has continued on its remarkable transition path from a state of high birth and death rates to one characterised by low birth and death rates. At the heart of that transition has been the growth in the number and proportion of older persons.

- Least Developed
- Less Developed
- More Developed

Source: United Nations Population Division

The ageing of the world's population

Over the past few years, the world's population has continued on its remarkable transition path from a state of high birth and death rates to one characterised by low birth and death rates. At the heart of that transition has been the growth in the number and proportion of older persons. Such a rapid, large and ubiquitous growth has never been seen in the history of civilisation.

The current demographic revolution is predicted to continue well into the coming centuries. Its major features include the following:

- One of every ten persons is now 60 years or above; by 2050, one out of five will be 60 years or older; and by 2150, one out of three persons will be 60 years or older.
- The older population itself is ageing. The increase in the number of very old people (aged 80+ years) is projected to grow by a factor of from 8 to 10 times on the global scale, between 1950 and 2050. Currently, the oldest old constitute 11 per cent of the population aged 60 and above. By 2150, about a third of the older population will be 80 years or older.

- The majority of older persons (55 per cent) are women. Among the oldest old (80 years or older), 65 per cent are women.
- Striking differences exist between regions. One out of five Europeans, but one out of twenty Africans, is 60 years or older.
- In some developed countries today, the proportion of older persons is close to one in five. During the first half of the next century that proportion will reach one in four and in some countries one in two
- As the tempo of ageing in developing countries is more rapid than in developed countries, developing countries will have less time than the developed countries to adapt to the consequences of population ageing.

- By the end of this century, the majority of the world's older persons (51 per cent) will be living in urban areas. It is projected that by the year 2000, almost 78 per cent of older women and more than 75 per cent of older men in more developed regions will be living in urban areas.

The majority of older persons of both sexes in developing regions are expected to remain rural (about 58 per cent of women and 60 per cent of men).

- At the individual level, it is estimated that more than 20 years will be added to the average life of an individual by the end of this century.
- The 1998 Revision of the United Nations population estimates and projections will for the first time disaggregate the population aged 80 years and above into ages 80-84, 85-89, 90-94, 95-99, and 100 and over.

This will mark the first time the international community will have consistent estimates and projections of the numbers of people in the oldest age groups for countries and areas of the world.

© United Nations / Division for Social Policy and Development

Percentage of the world population aged 60 and over 1950-2150, medium fertility scenario

The older population itself is ageing. The increase in the number of very old people (aged 80+) is projected to grow by a factor of from 8 to 10 times on the global scale, between 1950 and 2050. Currently, the oldest old constitute 11 per cent of the population aged 60 and above. By 2150, about a third of the older population will be 80 years or older.

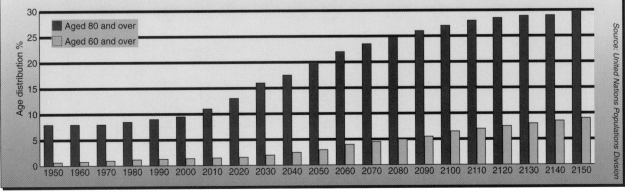

Source: United Nations Populations Division

Older women

Because of demographic, cultural and income differences between the genders, ageing means more challenges for women than for men

Women live longer than men

Nearly everywhere women live longer than men, so the older world is also a female world.

Globally, just over half of the older population aged 60-69 are women, but 65 per cent of those aged 80 years and over are women.

The double discrimination

Wherever they are, it is common for older people to be marginalised by their communities. In many places women are also denied opportunities, so the situation of older women can be doubly difficult. In childhood, girls often receive less nutrition, education and health care than boys.

This affects their health, economic status and earning potential in later life.

In Tanzania, for example, only five per cent of women aged 60 or over are literate compared to 27 per cent of men in the same age group.

Where women face discrimination, older women may lack representation and the chance to voice their opinions; and they may have limited chances to earn an income.

Widows

Women often marry men older than themselves and in many societies they are less likely than men to marry again if they are divorced or widowed.

For these reasons, women have a much higher chance of being widowed in later life than men. It has been said that widowhood is a fact of life for women over 75 in less-developed countries.

In Colombia 46 per cent of women aged 60 or over are widowed compared to 15 per cent of men in the same age group. In India 78 per cent of women aged 70 and over are widowed, compared to 27 per cent of men.

Unmarried or widowed women have a higher probability of living in poverty than women who are married. It can be much more difficult for a woman on her own to earn a living, especially if she lacks family support or lives in a community where the status of women is low.

Older women and health

Because girls and women may not receive adequate health care throughout their lives, women often have a greater risk of ill health in older age. Women's health may also be weakened by childbearing.

Work, pensions and poverty

In 1997, 58 per cent of older women lived in less-developed countries, but by 2025 it is estimated that this proportion will rise to 71 per cent. Because of the challenges faced by women as they age, older women are more likely to experience poverty than older men.

Older women are less likely to undertake paid work than older men. As well as this, where pension schemes do exist, women are less likely to be eligible to receive pensions. This is because if they have worked outside the home it is often in a low-paid and informal role.

Older women do many things to secure their livelihood. In many countries older women continue to work. In Thailand, for example, 43 per cent of women aged 60-64 are still working, as are 19 per cent of women aged over 65. These figures are deceptively low because older women – even more than older men – are likely to engage in work which is not in the formal employment sector and so is not recorded in official statistics.

HelpAge International has produced a booklet called *Older Women in Development* outlining the issues affecting older women in less-developed countries.

• The above is an extract from Helpage International's web site which can be found at http://www.oneworld.org/helpage

OVER 80's CLUB

UK lifespan 'is heading toward 80'

By Sarah Boseley,
Health Correspondent

Life expectancy throughout the world is improving so rapidly that within 25 years, half the babies born on the planet will live until they are 75, according to the annual World Health Organisation World Health Report, published yesterday.

In the West, our future is likely to be an increasingly long and healthy life, followed by a quick death, senior WHO scientists have revealed. The average Briton now expects to live to 77. By the year 2025, UK life expectancy will be 80.

Within five to ten years, each of us will have access to a genetic chip, which will spell out the potential physical weaknesses that could cause our demise, from inherited heart problems to cancer.

But while the rich nations benefit, the people of poor nations still face a perilous outlook, said Hiroshi Nakajima, director-general of the WHO. 'There are the many hundreds of millions of men, women and children still trapped in the grimmest poverty,' he said, 'where the burdens of ill health, disease and inequality are heaviest.'

Karol Sikora, head of the programme on cancer control in Lyon, France, said the future for the health of the wealthiest in the world was hidden in our genes.

'In five to 10 years' time we can start to look at diseases in the genetic background. Some are clearly inherited. Cancer and cardiovascular disease both have genetic components, but also environmental factors. People who have a genetic test will be given a tailored message on their lifestyle.'

A human genome project will be finished in about 2005. Once the map of our genes is complete, it will be possible to go to a GP for a mouth swab, which can then be processed by a computer. The computer will be able to identify any mutations in our genes which could lead to those diseases which can be inherited.

Armed with the complete genetic information, a doctor can suggest an improved lifestyle that would lower our risk of an early death.

> **The average Briton now expects to live to 77. By the year 2025, UK life expectancy will be 80**

The WHO's annual report, in the 50th year of its existence, looks at the remarkable progress made in the last half century and the state of things to come in the next 25 years. Life expectancy in the developed world has significantly outstripped the biblical three score years and ten.

'In the last 24 hours, 360,000 children have been born into the world and for the first time in human history, half will live until the age of 75,' said Dr Sikora.

Just as life expectancy in the UK will rise to 80, so it will in the United States. Some nations will enjoy even greater lifespans – but in the developing world, the picture will remain much grimmer. Ugandan life expectancy is now just 41 and in Mozambique it is 47.

The greatest enemies to a lively old age will be dementia and disability. Heart disease and stroke, which are largely preventable with better diet, will decline.

Alcohol has played a central part in the drastic decline in the health of the old Soviet Union, according to a report. There has been 'a catastrophic increase in mortality,' say Martin McKee and David Leon from the London School of Hygiene and Tropical Medicine.

Between 1987 and 1994, male life expectancy in the Russian Federation dropped by seven years, to 57.6 years. In some parts of the country it has fallen to 49.

© *The Guardian*
May, 1998

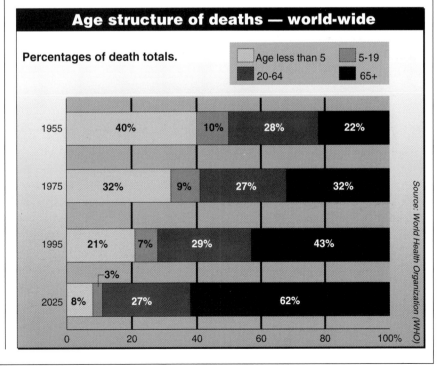

Age structure of deaths — world-wide

Percentages of death totals.

Legend: Age less than 5 | 5-19 | 20-64 | 65+

Year	Age less than 5	5-19	20-64	65+
1955	40%	10%	28%	22%
1975	32%	9%	27%	32%
1995	21%	7%	29%	43%
2025	8%	3%	27%	62%

Source: World Health Organization (WHO)

You're never too young to be old

How does it feel to be old? Twenty-five-year-old Alex Hayes put on goggles, ear plugs and a helpless manner and went to find out

When you are young and fit, it's hard to sympathise with the limitations of old age. Young people are more likely to seethe and rev their engines than to empathise with the little old lady wobbling slowly across the road.

With the aim of increasing understanding of the handicaps of old age, I have been muscled into taking part in Through Other Eyes – a scientific experiment to raise people's awareness of a very real social problem. In other words, show us how it actually feels to be old. I was escorted on this mission by Gaby Brooks and Sharon Steele of Age Concern.

Age Concern believes that most of the younger population have no idea how difficult it is for some elderly people to perform everyday tasks such as open a milk carton or shop, let alone deal with more arduous chores. 'Our ultimate aim is for people to realise how their mother or granny might feel,' explains Ms Steele. 'Once you see how your close relatives are struggling, your attitude towards the aged automatically changes. The next time you're at a supermarket till or behind a slow-moving elderly lady in the street, you're likely to show more patience.'

The experiment involves wearing ankle and wrist weights to simulate loss of strength and agility; putting on specially prepared goggles, to represent cataracts, tunnel vision and retina damage, and inserting ear plugs to reduce hearing.

According to the charity's research, 'the United Kingdom is an ageing society and, by the year 2026, half the adult population will be aged 55 or over. It is also significant that 80 per cent of the UK's private wealth is in the hands of people over 50, who are also the biggest spenders in every sector.' Significant because supermarkets, department stores and other services obviously need older buyers. Fail to accommodate their needs and you risk alienating a large share of your target audience. Ms Steele admits that the original reason for companies showing an interest in the scheme is economic. 'But, after their staff have done our workshop, their attitudes do change.'

At first all the contraptions make me feel very self-conscious and unsure. 'That's exactly how most old people feel,' Ms Steele points out. 'Many of them lose confidence when they go out, especially if they are in a foreign environment.' I certainly struggled. The weights (half a kilo around my wrist and one kilo around my ankle) weren't too cumbersome, but the inflatable orange armband did cut off the circulation in my arm. If I had had to carry shopping bags for any length of time, I would have found the experience difficult, if not impossible. The surgical gloves on each hand also made simple tasks more awkward, as did the goggles.

The combination of these two impairments was truly challenging. When paying for some flowers, which I could barely see, I struggled desperately to get change out of my pocket, let alone differentiate between the various coins.

Had my manner changed significantly when I was 'old'? 'You were definitely affected,' says Ms Steele. 'When you were buying the flowers, you cocked your head to hear the vendor clearly. And you crossed the street over-cautiously, even though the traffic had stopped.'

So will I now be more sympathetic towards older people? 'The aim of the workshop is not for people to feel sorry for the aged and tip-toe around them. A lot of them actually cope very well with their disabilities. What we're trying to say is that there's no need for some of the present barriers to be there.'

These 'barriers' are often small, seemingly insignificant obstacles, which prove insurmountable for the elderly. 'For example, the colour schemes that some organisations use to promote their products prevent older people from seeing the price on the tag. Another example is the excessive use of mirrors in shops. It can be very confusing and disorientating. These are artificial barriers; aesthetic additions which serve no practical purpose. I mean, why put a stair in a building if it's not needed?'

Age Concern has carried out its workshop in large companies such as Safeway and Nestlé. The workshops take half a day, cost between £595 and £895, and can accommodate a maximum of 12 people. And the scheme is making waves. Earlier this year, British Gas agreed to sponsor them. 'They give us money to develop the programme, market it and renew some of the equipment.'

On a personal level, my greatest achievement was threading a needle and sewing a button on to a piece of fabric despite my blurry vision and shaking hands. Now, for someone with a dreadful sewing record (one poorly sewn shirt-button in 25 years), this was no mean feat. Ironically, though – now that the contraptions have been removed – I will have to wait 40-odd years before I sew as expertly again. In the meantime, old people around Britain will continue raking it in on Bingo night. That's the injustice of being young.

• For further information about Age Concern, call 0800 00 99 66.

First published in The Independent September, 1998

A life in the South is 7 years longer

By Tim Knowles

A boy born in Cambridge can expect to live almost seven years longer than his counterpart in Manchester, researchers claimed yesterday.

Differences in life expectancy are still widening dramatically between the North and South, according to a major study.

And the longevity gap between rich and poor continues to grow, with men in affluent areas living four years longer than those in the most deprived districts.

Manchester comes bottom of the national league for life expectancy with men averaging less than 70 years, and women 76. Much of the rest of northern England fares little better.

Only North Yorkshire and South Cheshire make it into the top 50, out of 105 regions.

With the exception of three inner London areas, the regions with the lowest life expectancy are all in the North.

The longest-lived men are in Cambridge, while a woman in Bromley, Kent, which is top of the female league, can expect to live five years longer than a woman in Manchester.

The survey shows that despite advances in medical science, better diets and housing, the regional variations are wider now than 10 years ago. The figures reflect the link between lifestyle and health said Dr Veena Soni Raleigh, from the National Institute of Epidemiology at the University of Surrey, Guildford.

'It's important to recognise that poor health isn't just a question of getting a disease. It's a cumulative lifetime of disadvantage. You take one step down the ladder and the whole process accelerates. One has to target the problem on a number of fronts.'

Nationally, the average life expectancy for a man by the mid-1990s, from when the data was compiled, was 74. A decade earlier it was 72. For women it had risen from 77 to 79.

Of the top ten regions for male life expectancy, the most northerly is Solihull in the West Midlands.

© The Daily Mail
December, 1998

The top . . . the bottom

Figures are life expectancy per health area

	Males	Females		Males	Females
Cambridge	76.6	81.1	Leicestershire	74.7	79.9
Western Surrey	76.4	81.1	NW Anglia	74.6	79.8
Eastern Surrey	76.2	80.8	N Cumbria	73.3	78.8
Barnet	76.0	80.9	Sheffield	73.3	79.4
Solihull	76.0	80.6	W Yorkshire	73.2	75.5
NW Hertfordshire	75.9	80.6	Ealing, Hammersmith & Hounslow	73.2	79.7
Oxfordshire	75.9	80.9	Doncaster	73.2	78.5
Dorset	75.9	81.4	Walsall	73.1	78.1
Bromley	75.7	81.4	Rotherham	73.1	78.6
Suffolk	75.7	80.6	Bradford	72.9	78.5
N & Mid Hampshire	75.7	80.8	Wakefield	72.9	78.0
Exeter & N Devon	75.7	81.0	Coventry	72.9	78.7
SW Hertfordshire	75.7	80.6	S Durham	72.9	78.1
N Essex	75.6	80.4	Wigan & Bolton	72.8	77.8
E&N Hertfordshire	75.6	80.6	N Cheshire	72.8	78.0
Somerset	75.6	80.9	N Staffordshire	72.8	78.4
W Sussex	75.5	80.9	NW Lancashire	72.7	78.7
E Norfolk	75.5	80.7	Barnsley	72.7	78.1
Buckinghamshire	75.4	80.1	N Birmingham	72.6	78.3
Gloucestershire	75.4	80.5	S Birmingham	72.6	79.0
Kingston & Richmond	75.4	80.8	Wolverhampton	72.6	79.2
Herefordshire	75.3	80.6	Newcastle & N Tyneside	72.6	78.1
Southampton & SW Hampshire	75.3	80.8	N Durham	72.6	77.8
Berkshire	75.3	80.1	Bury and Rochdale	72.5	77.9
Bristol	75.2	80.5	E Lancashire	72.4	77.8
Wiltshire and Bath	75.2	80.3	Salford & Trafford	72.4	78.0
Hillingdon	75.1	80.1	St Helens and Knowsley	72.4	77.6
Brent and Harrow	75.1	80.7	Tees	72.2	77.8
Worcester	75.0	80.1	Sunderland	72.1	77.4
Cornwall & I. of Scilly	75.0	80.3	W Pennine	72.1	77.7
Huntingdon	75.0	80.5	Sandwell	72.0	78.3
N Yorkshire	74.9	80.1	South of Tyne	71.9	77.8
Croydon	74.9	79.8	Camden & Islington	71.8	78.8
E Sussex	74.9	80.6	SE London	71.7	78.4
W Kent	74.8	79.6	E London & the City	71.7	78.4
Plymouth & Torbay	74.8	80.6	Liverpool	71.2	77.3
E Kent	74.7	80.1	Manchester	69.9	76.7

Ageing process

Focus on healthy ageing

Why study the biology of ageing?

One of the greatest current challenges in medical science is to understand the ageing process in sufficient detail to allow us to open new paths to improving the quality of the later years of life. It is important to be clear that the goal is to improve the quality of life in old age rather than to extend the length of life, regardless of its quality.

All of us, if we live long enough, will experience aspects of ageing that will increase our frailty and limit our independence. But we do not all age in the same way. Some will remain free from disease for a very long time, whereas others will develop one or more of a range of age-related diseases.

So what is normal ageing and how is it related to the diseases of old age? Do different diseases share common causative mechanisms? Can these diseases be slowed or prevented by changes in nutrition or lifestyle, as well as by medical drugs?

What is ageing and why does it occur?

In one sense we all know what ageing is, although scientifically the mechanisms have been very hard to pin down. We used to think that ageing was programmed into us by some kind of death clock, but this view is no longer widely held.

We now think that ageing happens because during our lifetime the cells and tissues of our bodies accumulate many microscopic faults that eventually get in the way of normal functions. The good news is that if we can find ways to reduce this damage, or to increase the effectiveness of our natural repair systems, we might delay the onset of disease.

Cell ageing

Human cells from normal tissue can be propagated in the test tube, but eventually they stop growing, age and die. Cells grown from old donors divide less than cells from young donors; so there is good reason to believe that the study of cell ageing can throw light on the ageing of the body as a whole.

Research is identifying some of the factors that appear to control cell ageing. The cells that make up the organs of the body (e.g. brain, skin, bone) age in different ways and at different rates. However all cells have to cope with similar kinds of damage, and common factors may affect their ageing. Understanding the role of common factors in the development of different age-related diseases is a unique benefit that comes from studying the cellular basis of ageing. Work funded by Research into Ageing is examining how cells age.

Causes of ageing

The kinds of damage most likely to cause ageing are in the genetic material (DNA) of cells and the accumulation of altered cellular components. Altered proteins are important in diseases as diverse as Alzheimer's disease and cataract, while mutations play a part in cancers (many of which become commoner with age), and in muscle weakness.

Much of the damage arises as a by-product of normal living. For example, 1-2% of the oxygen we breathe gives rise to highly reactive molecules called free radicals, which can damage DNA and proteins. Our bodies have excellent natural protection against mutations and free radicals, which is why we live as long as we do, but some faults slip through.

The role of genetics

Genetic research is providing valuable clues to ageing and age-

related diseases. The fruit fly and soil nematode worm are helping to identify genes that affect life span. Many of these turn out to be genes that control maintenance and repair systems.

In humans, genes are being found that affect the risk of age-related diseases such as Alzheimer's disease and osteoarthritis.

Nutrition and lifestyle
Current understanding of the ageing process places a priority on good nutrition, because food fuels the natural repair systems, and provides the raw materials for healthy cell turnover. Low calorie intake in some animals has been shown to improve health in old age, but it is not known whether calorie restriction has the same effect in humans.

Exercise has clear benefits for health, as long as precautions are taken to avoid injury. Recent work has shown that regular exercise can slow the development of age-related decline in muscle.

The need for further research
Although much is known about the ageing process, we lack detailed knowledge of the precise mechanisms involved and how these contribute to age-associated disease. Basic ageing research is a relatively new field. Not only do we still need answers to these fundamental questions, but we also need to train dedicated young researchers. Our goal is a deeper understanding of the mechanisms responsible for infirmity and disease in old age, which can be used to enhance and extend quality of life. The scale of the task is immense.

How you can help us
Research into Ageing funds important research into the diseases and disabilities that commonly affect older people. The ageing process is one of our key areas of research. We receive no central funding from government for our research programme and have to rely on private, corporate and trust donations to continue our work.

- Research into Ageing wishes to thank Tom Kirkwood, Professor of Biological Gerontology at the University of Manchester, for his help in the preparation of this information.

© Research into Ageing

Population ageing – a public health challenge

By 2020 more than 1,000 million people aged 60 years and older will be living in the world, more than 700 million of them in developing countries

One of the main features of the world population in the 20th century has been a considerable increase in the absolute and relative numbers of older people in both developed and developing countries. This phenomenon is referred to as 'population ageing'.

- Of the approximately 580 million elderly people (60 years and more) in the world today, around 355 million live in developing countries.

  From a demographic point of view population ageing is a result of both mortality and fertility: fewer children are born and more people reach old age.

- Over the last fifty years mortality rates in developing countries have declined dramatically raising the average life expectancy at birth from around 41 years in the early 1950s to almost 62 years in 1990. By 2020, it is projected to reach 70 years.

- There are currently more than 20 developing countries, in which life expectancy at birth is 72 years or above. Among these are Costa Rica (77), Cuba (76), Jamaica (75), Argentina and Sri Lanka (73), Malaysia (72) and the Republic of Korea (72).

- More recently sharp falls have also occurred in birth rates in nearly all developing countries except for most of Sub-Saharan Africa. Total fertility rates in China, for example, declined from 5.5 in 1970 to the current 1.8 level. Respective figures for Brazil are 5.1 and 2.2 and for India 5.9 and 3.1.

  Population ageing has become an important development issue that requires urgent action. Projections into the first quarter of the 21st century, prepared independently by a number of organisations and scientists, merit the closest attention:

- By 2020 the number of elderly people world-wide will reach more than 1,000 million with over 700 million of them in developing countries.

- Over the next quarter-century, Europe is projected to retain its title of 'oldest' region in the world. Currently, elderly people represent around 20% of the total population now and will represent 25% by 2020.

- The 'oldest' country by 2020 will be Japan (31%), followed by Italy, Greece and Switzerland (above 28%). Today, the countries with the highest proportion of elderly people are Greece and Italy (both 23% in 1998).

- By 2020, the proportion of population aged 60 and over is projected to reach 23% in North America, 17% in East Asia, 12% in Latin America and 10% in South Asia.

- By 2020, of the ten countries with the largest elderly populations in the world, five will be in the developing world: China (230 million), India (142 million), Indonesia (29 million), Brazil (27 million) and Pakistan (18 million).

- In 2020, the proportion of 'oldest old' (80 years and older) in the above-60 group is projected to be 22% in Greece and Italy, 21% in Japan, France and Spain, and 20% in Germany. In several developing countries, including Uruguay, Cuba and Argentina, this proportion will be between 15% and 20%.

In developed countries, population ageing has evolved gradually as a result of an earlier decline in fertility and improving living standards for the majority of the population over a relatively long period of time after the industrial revolution. Technological breakthroughs in the field of medicine, including the development of new and effective drugs and vaccines, contributed to this process much later.

In developing countries, population ageing is occurring more rapidly because of rapid fertility decline and an increasing life expectancy due to medical interventions based on the use of advanced technology and drugs. These interventions have provided effective means to treat and prevent many diseases that used to kill people prematurely. Also of importance is the fact that population ageing in the developing world is accompanied by persistent poverty.

- In France, it has taken 115 years (1865-1980) for the proportion of the elderly population to approximately double from 7 to 17%. It is projected that in China it will take only 27 years between 2000 and 2027 for the proportion of the population aged 60 years and over to double from 10% to 20%.
- Between 1990 and 2025 the rate of increase in the number of the older people in developing countries is expected to be 7 to 8 times higher in countries such as Colombia, Malaysia, Kenya, Thailand and Ghana, as compared, for example, with the United Kingdom and Sweden.

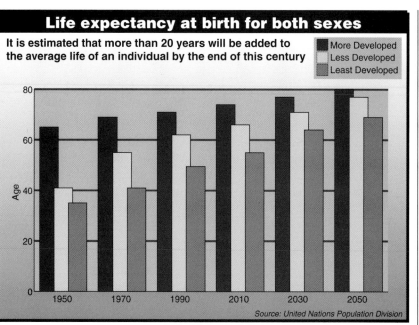

Life expectancy at birth for both sexes

It is estimated that more than 20 years will be added to the average life of an individual by the end of this century

More Developed
Less Developed
Least Developed

Source: United Nations Population Division

These developing countries are expected to experience an increase of between 200% and 300% in their elderly populations over a period of only 35 years.

The rapidly growing absolute and relative numbers of older people in both developed and developing countries mean that more and more people will be entering the age when the risk of developing certain chronic and debilitating diseases is significantly higher. As such, population ageing presents new and serious challenges for national and international public health.

By 2020, it is projected that three-quarters of all deaths in developing countries could be ageing-related.

The largest share of these deaths will be caused by non-communicable diseases (NCDs), such as diseases of the circulatory system (CSDs), cancers and diabetes.

- In Latin America, NCDs are on a steady increase. In Argentina, Cuba and Uruguay, for example, CSDs together with cancers are already responsible for more than 60% of all deaths. In Cuba, hypertension prevalence in men and women has reached 34.5% and 27.1%, while diabetes affects 5.7% of women and 2.9% of men.
- Population surveys in a number of African countries indicate that hypertension rates are on the rise, as is the prevalence of diabetes. In Seychelles, hypertension affects 22% of the population; in

South Africa – 16%; in Mauritius – 14%. Diabetes affects from 4 to 15% of the population in the three countries.

- In parts of Asia, CSDs and cancers are now the two leading groups of causes of mortality. Hypertension has been found in India, Indonesia and Thailand to affect up to 15% of the adult population. Diabetes reaches industrialised-country proportions in urban populations.
- NCDs have a major impact on health economics. According to the American Heart Association, in 1996, cardiovascular diseases in the USA cost $151.3 billion, including medical treatment and lost productivity from disability.
- Diabetes mellitus alone, which is estimated to affect some 143 million people world-wide, claims on an average around 8% of total health budgets in industrialised countries.

Population ageing has also been projected to aggravate the magnitude of mental health problems. This will happen because of the increasing life expectancy of those with mental disorders and an ever-growing number of people reaching the age at which the risk of such disorders is high.

- Estimated at 29 million today, the number of people affected by senile dementia in Africa, Asia and Latin America may exceed 55 million in 2020.

© WHO/OMS, 1999

The UN principles for older persons

Independence

1. Older persons should have access to adequate food, water, shelter, clothing and health care through the provision of income, family and community support and self-help.
2. Older persons should have the opportunity to work or to have access to other income-generating opportunities.
3. Older persons should be able to participate in determining when and at what pace withdrawal from the labour force takes place.
4. Older persons should have access to appropriate educational and training programmes.
5. Older persons should be able to live in environments that are safe and adaptable to personal preferences and changing capacities.
6. Older persons should be able to reside at home for as long as possible.

Participation

7. Older persons should remain integrated in society, participate actively in the formulation and implementation of policies that directly affect their well-being and share their knowledge and skills with younger generations.
8. Older persons should be able to seek and develop opportunities for service to the community and to serve as volunteers in positions appropriate to their interests and capabilities.
9. Older persons should be able to form movements or associations of older persons.

Care

10. Older persons should benefit from family and community care and protection in accordance with each society's system of cultural values.
11. Older persons should have access to health care to help them to maintain or regain the optimum level of physical, mental and emotional well-being and to prevent or delay the onset of illness.
12. Older persons should have access to social and legal services to enhance their autonomy, protection and care.
13. Older persons should be able to utilise appropriate levels of institutional care providing protection, rehabilitation and social and mental stimulation in a humane and secure environment.
14. Older persons should be able to enjoy human rights and fundamental freedoms when residing in any shelter, care or treatment facility, including full respect for their dignity, beliefs, needs and privacy and for the right to make decisions about their care and the quality of their lives.

Self-fulfilment

15. Older persons should be able to pursue opportunities for the full development of their potential.
16. Older persons should have access to the educational, cultural, spiritual and recreational resources of society.

Dignity

17. Older persons should be able to live in dignity and security and be free of exploitation and physical or mental abuse.
18. Older persons should be treated fairly regardless of age, gender, racial or ethnic background, disability or other status, and be valued independently of their economic contribution.

© United Nations – Department of
Public Information, New York

Pensions timebomb

Eight million face retirement in poverty because they are not saving money now

Eight million workers are failing to save for their retirement, a shock report reveals.

Six out of ten families – including half the self-employed – are making no provision towards their pensions.

Thousands of people now in their 30s will be left to survive on the basic state benefit, which will be worth less than a third of average earnings, warns the 172-page review.

'The report sounds a clear warning that many people face a big drop in their income when they come to retire,' said Social Security Secretary Harriet Harman.

The Government plans to tackle the problem by creating a new 'stakeholder' second pension.

Under the plan, to be unveiled in a Green Paper later this year, those not in a company or private pension will have part of their salary compulsorily paid into the system. This would guarantee that everyone gets more than the basic state pension.

However, the man in charge of the independent review, Tom Ross, warned yesterday that the middle classes could be forced to pay more into the scheme to subsidise three million poor.

The plan would involve 're-distribution from the better-off people to the not so well-off', said Mr Ross, a City pensions consultant.

The problem is funding the so-called citizenship pension for those earning below £9,000 a year, carers, and others unable to contribute. One option would be to slot the low-paid into the existing State Earnings Related Pension Scheme, or Serps.

This would defer the problem, as the money to pay the pensions would not have to be found until they retired.

However, Labour has said it intends to retain Serps – which provides a small top-up income above the basic state pension – for only four more years.

By Paul Eastham, Political Correspondent

Another way of raising the money – by increasing taxes – would fly in the face of General Election promises.

The only other real option is to create a special fund to help the poor – most probably from contributions of the better-off. Legal and General has estimated that someone on average earnings of £18,000 a year would have to invest a tenth of that to ensure they receive two-thirds of their income on retirement.

That figure would have to rise to fund the citizenship pensions.

One of the eight-strong Pensions Provision Group, which wrote the report, said: 'If there were to be a fund for everyone which required people to pay in while they are working then it does mean there would have to be redistribution from the better-off to pay the contributions of the low-paid.'

A source close to the Health Department declined to discuss what role 'redistribution' would play in funding the new pension schemes.

He said it was 'too-close' to the publication of the pensions Green Paper to discuss the Secretary of State's plans.

But he said Miss Harman was likely to use a 'variety of means' to ensure that pensioners no longer fell into the trap of having to claim means-tested benefits – and got the chance to save more for their retirement.

The review was set up by the Government last summer. Miss Harman assembled a group of experts from the City, TUC, academia and charity and asked them to find out how many people had inadequate pensions.

The group found that eight million were saving nothing, including half the 3.5 million self-employed.

By 2025 half of all pensioners will have incomes less than a third of average earnings, it said.

The gap between the richest and the poorest will grow, with the top people four times better off than those at the bottom.

Even today, one in five of those who retire see their incomes halved, the review said.

© The Daily Mail
June, 1998

Current pension scheme membership by age and sex

Pension scheme members. Employees aged 16 and over excluding YT and ET. Great Britain, 1996

Age	16-17	18-24	25-34	35-44	45-54	55+	Total
Men full-time							
Occupational pension*	[5]	23	53	69	71	59	58
Personal pension	[0]	16	35	28	23	17	26
Any pension	[5]	36	77	84	84	70	75
Women full-time							
Occupational pension*	†	27	56	64	61	58	53
Personal pension	†	9	24	22	15	12	18
Any pension	†	34	72	76	70	65	65
Bases = 100%							
Men full-time	43	426	1108	1078	906	376	3937
Women full-time	15	370	677	487	458	136	2143
Women part-time	87	156	405	523	470	267	1908

* Including a few people who were not sure if they were in a scheme but thought it possible
† Base too small to enable reliable analysis to be made

Source: General Household Survey

Income

The State Retirement Pension and other benefits

The amount of State Retirement Pension people receive when they retire depends on the amount of National Insurance (NI) contributions they paid during their working life, and on whether they made extra contributions, for example through the state earnings-related pension scheme (SERPS). Some people will get the basic pension, those who paid higher contributions will get more, and some will only get a proportion of the pension, if they did not pay full NI contributions for the requisite number of years.

- The basic State Retirement Pension April 1998-99

Single: £64.70 per week (man 65+ or woman 60+ who paid full contributions)
Couple: £103.40 per week, composed of:
£64.70 per week (for the husband)
£38.70 per week (for a wife who did not pay contributions herself)

- How many people in Great Britain receive a State Retirement Pension?

In September 1997 10,709,300 people were receiving the State Retirement Pension. This includes British pensioners living abroad (*Social Security Statistics* 1998, table B1.01).

- How many pensioners also receive Income Support?

'Income Support' is a means-tested benefit which assists people on low incomes. It supplements whatever income a person receives in order to bring it up to a fixed minimum level (known as an 'applicable amount'). This basic level may include 'premiums', making it higher for such groups as pensioners and disabled people.

In May 1997, 1.7 million people aged 60+ in Great Britain received Income Support, providing for more than 2 million people (recipients and their partners/dependants.) Of these, 1.5 million were retirement pensioners, or dependent on a retirement pensioner (*Social Security Statistics* 1998, tables A2.09 and A2.23).

It is estimated by the government that only between 61% and 70% of pensioners actually claim the Income Support to which they are entitled. This suggests that from 650,000 to as many as 950,000 pensioners may be eligible for Income Support, but are not claiming it. This is a particular problem among single female pensioners. It is estimated that only between 59% and 65% of single female pensioners claim the Income Support to which they are entitled. (Income Related Benefits: estimates of take up in 1996-7).

- Current levels of Income Support April 1998 - April 1999

The table overleaf ('Current levels of Income Support') shows the 'applicable amounts' used for calculating Income Support entitlement in the year 1998-9. Anyone whose income falls below these amounts, and who doesn't have considerable capital or savings, should receive the difference through an Income Support payment.

A comparison with the figures for the basic pension shows that the basic pension, both for single people and for couples, is below the Income Support applicable amount for people aged 60 or over. Everyone whose sole income is the basic pension is therefore eligible to claim Income Support.

- Number of pensioners in Great Britain receiving Housing Benefit and Council Tax Benefit

People who receive Income Support

are automatically entitled to claim Housing Benefit, to help cover the cost of renting their home, and Council Tax Benefit to cover any council tax they are liable to pay. People whose incomes are low, but not quite as low as the Income Support levels, may still be able to get some help with their rent and council tax under the Housing Benefit and Council Tax Benefit schemes.

The number of pensioners whose income is only just above the Income Support level is demonstrated by the fact that in 1997 in Great Britain more than 1.3 million pensioner households (that is, pensioners and their partners/dependants) received help with their council tax and 920,000 pensioner households received help with their rent, even though they were not eligible for Income Support (*Social Security Statistics* 1998, tables A3.04 and A4.03).

Other sources of pensioners' incomes

Pensioners' incomes derive from four main sources: social security benefits (this includes the State Retirement Pension, means-tested benefits such as Income Support and Housing Benefit, and sickness and disability

benefits), occupational pensions, savings and investments and employment earnings.

The table below ('The sources of pensioners' gross incomes') shows how the relative importance of these sources has changed over the last twenty years. The figures relate to the total income going to pensioners in the UK, not to the composition of individual pensioners' incomes.

It is clear from the table that the most dramatic change over the last twenty years is the fall in employment earnings. This is linked with the trend towards early retirement: only 43% of men aged between 60 and 64 were still 'economically active' in 1994, compared with 84% of men in 1975 (*GHS* 1996, table 5.8).

Occupational pensions have increased in importance as a source of income; this increase may be explained by the growing percentage of pensioners who have an occupational pension.

The relative importance of social security benefits has been decreasing gradually from 1979 onwards. Despite this decrease, however, benefits are still the largest source of pensioners' incomes. For 51% of the UK's pensioners, state benefits constitute 75% or more of their income (*Hansard*, 10.02.97) and for 70% of the UK's pensioners, state benefits constitute at least 50% of their income (*Hansard*, 6.12.93, col 112). The rates set by government for State Retirement Pensions and other benefits have, therefore, an enormous impact on the living standards of the retired population.

- How many pensioners have sources of income besides state benefits?

The figures given in the table below ('The sources of pensioners' gross incomes') refer to the overall income going to pen-sioners, but the various sources of income are, of course, not evenly divided amongst individual pension-ers. In 1995/96, 64% of pensioner households had an occupational pension and 74% had some form of income from savings (*Social Security Statistics* 1998, table B2.06 and B2.07). The size of these occupational pensions, however, is often very low.

© *Help the Aged*

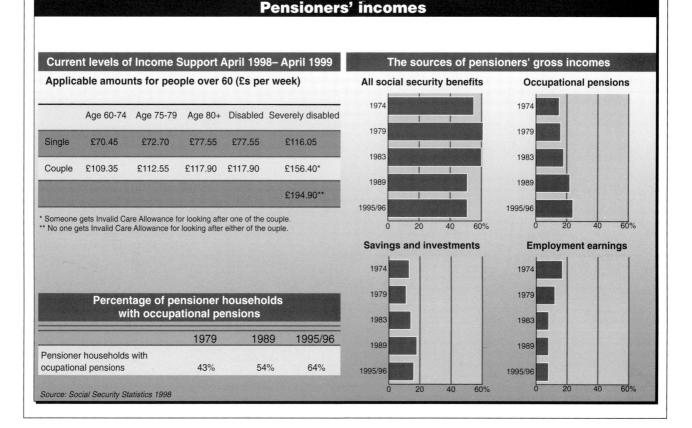

Pensioners' incomes

Current levels of Income Support April 1998– April 1999

Applicable amounts for people over 60 (£s per week)

	Age 60-74	Age 75-79	Age 80+	Disabled	Severely disabled
Single	£70.45	£72.70	£77.55	£77.55	£116.05
Couple	£109.35	£112.55	£117.90	£117.90	£156.40*
					£194.90**

* Someone gets Invalid Care Allowance for looking after one of the couple.
** No one gets Invalid Care Allowance for looking after either of the ouple.

Percentage of pensioner households with occupational pensions

	1979	1989	1995/96
Pensioner households with ocupational pensions	43%	54%	64%

Source: Social Security Statistics 1998

The sources of pensioners' gross incomes

All social security benefits
1974, 1979, 1983, 1989, 1995/96 — 0, 20, 40, 60%

Occupational pensions
1974, 1979, 1983, 1989, 1995/96 — 0, 20, 40, 60%

Savings and investments
1974, 1979, 1983, 1989, 1995/96 — 0, 20, 40, 60%

Employment earnings
1974, 1979, 1983, 1989, 1995/96 — 0, 20, 40, 60%

Age – the issues for today's workplace

- Employment law already allows for age discrimination to be challenged, but the introduction of a Code of Practice in the UK in 1999, coupled with increasing concern about age in Europe, guarantees that this issue will remain high on the employment agenda.

- The EFA is currently involved in the consultation process on the development of the Code of Practice. The Code is now going through a process of public consultation and will be implemented in the spring of 1999. The Minister announced the introduction of a Code as a measure to tackle the unfairness of age discrimination. The Code will be fully evaluated by 2001 so that the Government may monitor its effectiveness 'in challenging stereotypes within employment practices and promoting an age-diverse-workforce'.

- Many employers have yet to grasp that there has been a significant demographic shift in the population. The population is ageing, but from an employment (rather than a marketing) perspective it is the dramatic drop in numbers of young people coming into the labour market which will have the greatest impact. The last recession masked the large fall in 16-24-year-olds which took place between 1986 and 1996. The numbers of 25-34-year-olds is now dropping to the same extent.

- A number of sectors and areas are now reporting difficulty in recruiting and in some cases retaining staff. There are undoubtedly shortages of skilled people but the employment statistics clearly show that in many areas there are also large numbers of unemployed or inactive over-45s.

- As organisations have become more decentralised and less hierarchical, responsibility for employment decisions has become devolved. EFA research shows that line manager prejudice and the use of age as a shorthand in the decision-making process is a major factor in continuing poor practice.

- Ageism is still widespread. Some define an older worker as a 'woman over 35 and a man over 42'. EFA research shows that ageism affects all age groups and that half of those who have experienced ageism feel it was because they were 'too young'.

- Age discrimination affects all aspects of employment, not just recruitment. EFA research clearly shows that promotion, training as well as redundancy and retirement selection can all be affected when decisions are based on age.

- The business benefits of a mixed age workforce are now widely recognised. There is clear evidence that both turnover and absenteeism are reduced and that motivation and commitment are improved in organisations employing people of all ages.

- Recent research has highlighted the higher level of personal and communication skills that older workers can bring to the workplace and the business benefit that can be gained from 'reflecting your market'.

- There is no evidence that older workers cannot be trained or grasp new technology. 'Old dogs can learn new tricks' and also make excellent trainers and mentors.

- Becoming 'an employer of choice' is now essential so that organisations can effectively compete in the new labour market and into the new millennium.

The EFA does not promote positive discrimination in favour of older workers. Nor does it advocate employing older workers instead of younger workers.

EFA member companies recognise that a diversity of ages will help them compete more effectively in a rapidly changing and ageing market.

© Employers' Forum on Age (EFA)

Age discrimination

Key facts and guidance for managers

Definition

Age discrimination occurs when employers make decisions affecting procedures for advertising, recruitment, selection, promotion, training and development on the basis of individuals' age rather than their skills, abilities, qualifications and potential.

- Much research is concerned with discrimination against the over-50s but job adverts frequently give age limits of 40, 35 or even 30.

Background

- As the sex and race discrimination legislation of the 1970s and 1980s has become more widely accepted, people have become more aware of those groups which are not legally covered, i.e. older workers and people with disabilities.

  Reasons for age discrimination are:

- Recession – organisations' reductions in the size of the workforce concentrated on early retirement first and targeted redundancy at older workers.
- Younger workers are generally cheaper to employ.
- Young employees are thought to be more flexible, more skilled in technology.
- Older workers are thought to be more costly for benefits, such as sick leave and pensions as well as salary.

  However, organisations are now beginning to see the results of age discrimination:

- When older workers leave, their knowledge, skills and experience go too.
- Older employees tend to stay longer, give greater commitment and loyalty and have less absenteeism.
- Mixed age groups provide balance.
- Older customers, clients and suppliers may prefer dealing with older employees in retail, insurance, banking and other service industries.

Key facts

By the year 2050 almost a quarter of the population will be aged over 65. Yet economic activity rates for those over 50 are declining. According to government statistics:

- For men aged 50 to 64 the activity rate was 68.4% in 1995 (in 1975 the rate for men aged 55 to 59 was 94%).
- For women aged 50 to 59 in 1995 the rate was 63.9% but these rates are not declining – due perhaps to the increase in job opportunities, particularly part time, for women.
- Rates for those over retirement age drop dramatically: men – 9%, married women – 5%; and non-married women – 3%.
- Of those who do work, older people are more likely to work part time. In 1994:
- Of those aged 50 to 59 more than a quarter of those who worked were part time.
- Of those aged 60 to 64, 35.5% were part time.
- For the over-65s, 70.4% were part time.
- Older people are more likely to be self-employed: of those aged 50 to state pension age, 17% were self-employed (all employees: 12.8%).
- A study of 4,000 job adverts by Industrial Relations Services in 1993 found that almost one-third required applicants to be 45 or under. Some specified 35 or under.
- A study of the views of candidates and employers by Sanders & Sidney revealed that candidates believed career prospects started to be limited at age 42.
- The cost of replacement: W H Smith calculates that it costs £2,500 to replace a sales assistant.
- B & Q which decided to staff an entire store with over-50s as an

experiment to demonstrate the capabilities of older employees, found that staff turnover was six times lower than average, absenteeism was 39% lower and profitability turnover was up 18%. B&Q continues to recruit older workers but into mixed age group stores.

State of play

- There is no direct legislation on age discrimination in the UK. However, age-based selection for redundancy has been found to be unlawful (Walker, Nolan and Kiddy v Carbodies Ltd) and an age limit affecting more of one sex than the other could be seen as indirect discrimination under the Sex Discrimination Act 1975.
- About 100 large UK companies joined the Third Age Programme (organised by the Carnegie Foundation). Of these 20 have formally changed policies to end age discrimination.
- The Employers' Forum on Age (EFA) was set up in 1996. It is a network for employers to promote mixed aged workforces. The Industrial Society is a founder member. It provides information, auditing methods, research and so on.
- The POPE Project (People of previous experience) was set up by the Bradford & District TEC to help the unemployed over-50s get jobs. It created a register of such people and a list of employers with suitable vacancies. It matched candidates with available jobs and paid employers £2,000 for each job filled. In a year it made 110 placements.
- The age limit has now been dropped to 40, people have been given support and training and employers no longer receive the subsidy.

Best practice guidelines

Age discrimination reduces an organisation's effectiveness and, with a growing older population, gives a bad image.

- Recruitment policy should be to recruit the best staff, regardless of age. Organisations' employees should reflect the diversity of their existing and potential customers.
- To retain knowledge and experience the organisation needs to attract and retain a proportion of older employees.
- Reorganisations and redundancies should be planned so that appropriate, and not just older employees are targeted.
- Recruitment, training, development and promotion should be on the basis of experience and aptitude, not age.

- Challenge stereotypes – many older workers like computers, welcome a challenge and want to try something new.
- Capitalise on investments in training and development for employees in all age groups.
- Avoid 'ghettoes' of older workers – create mixed-age teams.
- Make sure that guidelines, policies and vision statements reflect the organisation's positive approach to age.

Industrial Society help

Publications:

- *Managing Best Practice* No 14: Managing Diversity.
- *Valuing Maturity* – a report on the employment of mature managers.

From the Industrial Society Library:

- *Getting on* – government document SEPC 1 Room 343.
- *Too old – who says?* (Advice for older workers) government document PL9 49.
- *Age and Employment* (book) by Richard Worsley, Age Concern, tel 0181 679 1075.
- EFA details, tel 0181 679 1075.

For further information on the topic covered in this information, please contact: The Industrial Society Information Service on 0171 262 2401.

Age discrimination in job applications — 'too old'

As the graph below shows, the perception of job applications having been affected by discrimination on the grounds of being too old were higher among men than women, and generally lower for those aged 60 or over. Just 7% of both men and women aged 50 to 54 believed they had been affected by discrimination for being too old when making a job application. Among those aged 45-69 who perceived experiencing age discrimination, 57% were men.

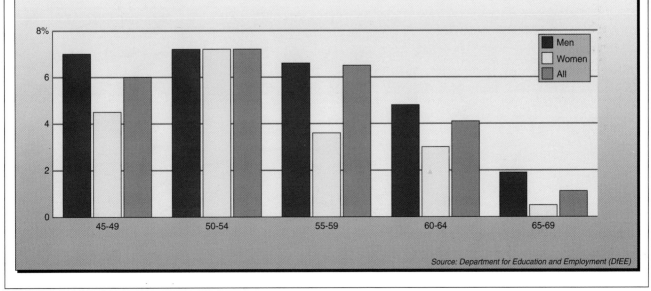

Source: Department for Education and Employment (DfEE)

Age prejudice 'costs Britain £26bn a year'

Employment rights: four million older workers are out of jobs, and the skills of millions more are underused

By Glenda Cooper, Social Affairs Correspondent

Workers who find themselves discriminated against because of their age may soon be able to take their grievance to industrial tribunals.

As the Government launched its code of practice against age discrimination yesterday, a report by the Employers' Forum on Age claimed that the practice cost the economy £26bn a year. In eight years, it is estimated, one-quarter of the working population will be over 50 but while there are now 9.3 million people in Britain aged 50-64, 3.7 million of them are not working.

The draft code, which businesses will be asked to follow from next year, covers recruitment, retirement and promotion, and urges employers to treat staff according to ability, not age. The Employment Minister, Andrew Smith, said he would consult the heads of industrial tribunals over the possibility of age-related cases being heard.

But charities for older people said that the new code of practice was 'unimpressive' and signalled a retreat by the Government from legislation.

Mr Smith said legislation had not been ruled out but he warned that it would be complicated. Other countries, such as the United States, New Zealand and France, had run into problems.

'The code is a big step forward in tackling age discrimination because it will establish new standards,' he said. 'Customers and workers will have a basis to complain to a company and to the wider forum of public opinion. The more widely the code is accepted, the more appropriate it will be for industrial tribunals to take account of it.'

The new code urges companies not to use age limits or phrases such as 'young graduates' in job advertisements, to use interviewing panels of mixed age and to promote staff on merit, irrespective of age.

The charity Age Concern welcomed the code as an important first step, but added that only legislation would get rid of ageism. 'With a recession predicted next year, even more older people will be in fear of losing their jobs and never working again. These people need to know that the law is on their side,' Age Concern's director-general, Sally Greengross, said.

Mervyn Kohler, head of public affairs at Help the Aged, said the move would contribute to consultation as it was 'the only show in town. But we have real worries about the code and feel it is a very unimpressive start,' he said. 'We need proper laws to tackle discrimination.'

Debra Allcock, of the Industrial Society, said the voluntary codes usually worked better than legislation in the long run because people were more likely to respond well to them. But, she added: 'What legislation can do is get people thinking about the issue, as was the case over equal opportunities.'

She said the priority for the Government should be to push education to make people aware that ageism was unacceptable.

Helen Garner, campaigns director for the Employers' Forum on Age, said the code was a start. 'But I think it will need strong support from the Government to work,' she said. 'They need to put funds into monitoring it and making sure all their departments and policies reflect the code.'

YOU MUST BE AWARE, MISTER JONES, THAT YOUR THIRTY YEARS EXPERIENCE DOES PUT YOU AT A CERTAIN DISADVANTAGE...

Appointments Board

Ken Pyne

Director left on shelf to stack shelves

As a computer sales director Tony Webster commanded a salary of £40,000 a year. Now he earns just £7,000 as a shelf-stacker for his local supermarket.

For more than 30 years Mr Webster, 59, worked in computers – designing hardware and software as well as working in sales – but his age means that since he was made redundant from his last job he has not been able to get full-time employment in this field.

He took his last employer to an industrial tribunal and won an out-of-court settlement for wrongful dismissal and breach of contract. He is convinced that ageism lay behind the loss of his job.

'The company I worked for was run by a 29-year-old. He said to me that he was worried that the average age of the company was creeping up. I was far older than anyone else, most of the rest were under 30,' Mr Webster said.

'Managers are worried by your age down on the sheet instead of looking at your ability'

'Soon afterwards I was given the sack.'

He feels this is not an isolated incident. Two years ago Mr Webster sent out 40 letters applying for jobs without mentioning his age. He received 29 replies and was invited to 12 interviews. When he mentioned his age on application letters, he never got a reply.

'I have a lot of experience, a lot of knowledge,' he said. 'The attitude is often that managers are worried by your age down on the sheet instead of looking at your ability.

'While I defend the right of employers to employ who they like, I feel angry about being ignored purely because of my age.'

To support himself, Mr Webster got a job at a Budgen supermarket, where he is paid £3.83 an hour to stack shelves. 'Though I like what I'm doing at the moment I would love to go back to computers,' he said.

'I can see that employers would be worried about the health aspect of employing older workers, but I'm doing a hard physical job at the supermarket. I've lost a stone and a half, so I can do anything. I've proved I've got stamina.'

Mr Webster is also doing some Web design part time and has continued to write poetry and short stories, some of which have been published. He feels he still has a lot to give to society.

'Older people often have a lot of loyalty and a lot of reliability,' he said. 'They have the ability to interact with other people. We need to educate employers into seeing the benefits of older employees – they still have so much to offer.'

© *The Independent*
November, 1998

The real cost of ageism

Information from Employers' Forum on Age (EFA)

An authoritative new report by the Employers' Forum on Age (EFA) has revealed for the first time the true cost of ageism to the UK economy.

The bill amounts to a staggering £26 billion each year – the equivalent of one-fifth of the country's GDP over the next five years.

A *profits warning: the macroeconomic costs of ageism* takes an in-depth look at the economic impact of ageism in the UK. The implications are vast – it can be argued that the country would not be facing a funding crisis for its hospitals, schools and transport systems if it did not continue to ignore the productive resources of older workers.

Of the 9.3 million people aged between 50 and 64 in the UK today, some 3.7 million are not in work. Most of these (3.4 million) are classified as 'economically inactive'

– not currently available or seeking work.

A *profits warning* argues that buried within these figures is a hidden workforce, excluded from official unemployment figures and largely rejected by employers. Currently, the number of inactive people aged between 50 and 64 is double the unemployment number for the entire country.

The £26 billion figure has been arrived at by calculating the potential contribution to the economy of the approximately 1 million 'economically inactive' over-50s who would be willing and capable of re-entering the workforce.

'We have come to view our ageing workforce as a burden and not an asset,' says Helen Garner, campaigns director of the EFA. 'But this ignorance and prejudice is costing us dear, both economically and socially.'

Séan Rickard, economist and author of A *profits warning*, says: 'The true cost to the nation of economically inactive older workers is not the dependency ratio (how many people each employee is supporting via their taxes) but the loss of goods and services that would have been produced.

'The challenge facing the nation is to restore the number of inactive people aged between 50 and 64 to the levels of 20 years ago.'

A *profits warning* highlights our failure as a nation to make full use of our productive resources – in this case people aged 50 and above. The report costs £35 (free to EFA members).

• The above is an extract from *Newsline*, produced by the Employers' Forum on Age. See page 41 for address details.

© *Employers' Forum on Age (EFA)*
December, 1998

Ministers outlaw age limits on jobs

**By Paul Waugh,
Political Correspondent**

The Government is to ban age limits on all vacancies in Job Centres as part of a drive to tackle age discrimination by employers.

The Employment Minister, Andrew Smith, announced the move when he unveiled plans for a business code of practice to remove ageism from the workplace. However, the code will only be voluntary and charities and MPs repeated their call for legislation to prosecute firms that refused to hire people because they were too young or too old.

Mr Smith did not rule out the idea of anti-discrimination laws, but made clear that the Government believed that the rising number of workers over 50 would soon force employers to change their ways. A quarter of all employees will be aged 50 or over by the year 2006 and no business could afford to ignore such a growing sector of the workforce, he said.

A report published yesterday by the Department for Education and Employment stated that those over 50 suffered the worst discrimination when it came to getting and keeping a job. The voluntary code of practice – which is to be published in the autumn following consultation with industry, unions and age charities – could form a 'soft law' in industrial tribunals, Mr Smith said. Even people in their 40s were experiencing discrimination, and it was important to send a message to employers that age prejudice was unacceptable, he added.

As a first step, the Government is removing upper age limits from all job advertisements in Job Centres. If any jobless person is turned down at interview stage because of their age, Job Centres will also stop using that firm's vacancy adverts.

'While this initiative will not in itself eliminate age discrimination in employment, the Government believes it is a positive step which will send a clear signal to employers about our commitment to assist older workers,' the report states. The New Deal programme will also be used to help older unemployed people into jobs.

Mr Smith said it was important to challenge the assumption that it was cheaper and more effective to employ a younger person.

'There are firms like B&Q who have recognised very positively the benefits to their operation, to their customers, as well as the benefits to employees of actually having an age diverse workforce – older workers working alongside younger workers in a way that works very successfully,' he said.

Age Concern England said the new code was a good start, but it could easily be ignored by bad employers and had ultimately to be backed up by legislation.

'It is vital that adequate provisions are made to ensure that no person is discriminated against on the grounds of age,' said director-general Sally Greengross.

Labour MP Linda Perham, who tried unsuccessfully to introduce a Private Member's Bill to outlaw ageism, said that while the code and Job Centre move in particular were welcome, legislation was vital.

'The United States have had laws on this since 1967. There are other countries in Europe and Australasia where they are in force and yet here we have no law at all,' she said. 'The Government says this is a complex area, but that was the excuse that was used to try to halt legislation banning discrimination on grounds of race and sex.'

The CBI claimed that the voluntary code would be more effective than legislation such as that proposed by Ms Perham. 'It would be unworkable, ineffective and would prove an unnecessary burden on business. There is little evidence from other countries that such legislation works,' they said.

How we are ageing

- In 1951, there were 300 people in the UK aged over 100. In 2031, there will be 34,00.

- By 2006, the largest group of the working population, 24 per cent, will be aged between 55 and 64.

- From 1991 to 2011, the number of people aged between 45 and 54 is set to increase by 2.3 million.

- In 1900, average life expectancy in this country was 50. By 1993 it had risen to 77 for men and 81 for women.

- In the United States, laws prohibit discrimination against anyone over 40, with no upper age limit for filing a claim.

- Supermarkets, fastfood restaurants and DIY stores are recruiting older workers because of longer opening hours.

- Researchers have claimed that people aged over 47 work more effectively than younger colleagues in the morning.

- A 1997 survey revealed that four out of five workers over 50 believed they had suffered age discrimination.

- Anti-ageism campaigners claim that older workers are more loyal to their employers and take less time off.

- In 1968, there were four people of working age funding the pension of each pensioner. By 2040, this will be down to two people per pensioner.

© The Independent
August, 1998

Don't snub the golden oldies, bosses urged

By David Norris, Industrial Correspondent

The Government yesterday launched a major drive to help Britain's growing army of older people get back to work.

Thousands of over-50s find they are turned down because of their age when they try to get jobs.

A poll earlier this year found that 18million people said they had experienced some form of age discrimination.

'It is absurd,' said Employment Minister Andrew Smith yesterday. 'Our message is that this country simply cannot afford to throw away their talents.'

Mr Smith is drawing up a new Code of Good Practice urging firms not to snub older workers, but to harness their experience and skills.

The code, to be published this autumn, will be seen as a poor second best by campaigners who wanted legislation to outlaw ageism at work. But Mr Smith said that, although laws had not been ruled out, the belief now was that they would be too complex and some employers would find ways to outflank them.

The voluntary code would be 'an early and positive way forward', he added.

He pointed out that employers who do discriminate on the grounds of age would soon have to change their tune anyway.

With people living longer and staying fitter, by 2006 more than a quarter of the UK's workforce would be 50 or over, Mr Smith went on. Separate statistics show that the number of people aged between 55 and 64 will rocket from 5.6 million now to 8.4 million in 2021, with many wanting to continue in work.

> **'It is absurd. Our message is that this country simply cannot afford to throw away their talents'**

The battle may, in fact, already be going the way of the old guard. A growing number of firms are actively recruiting pensioners because they find customers like their maturity and experience.

One is DIY chain B&Q which has been operating such a policy for some time. Another is pizza delivery firm Domino's. 'We find that older people are reliable, efficient and courteous to the public,' said finance director Stephen Hemsley last night.

'Around 80 per cent of our business is on the doorstep, so our delivery staff are often the only face of our company that people see.'

However, there is evidence that many big companies will stick to their present set retirement ages despite Government exhortations to change them.

One is BT, which retires staff at the age of 60. A spokesman said: 'We have a good pension scheme and people know about the retirement age when they join us. There is no problem.'

Last night, the charity Age Concern welcomed the Government's initiative. 'It is vital that adequate provisions are made to ensure that no person is discriminated against on the grounds of age,' said director-general Sally Greengross.

Earlier this year, the organisation mounted a poster campaign using a 56-year-old model to mimic the pose adopted by Eva Herzigova in the Wonderbra adverts.

The message was that the oldies were up to any job.

© The Daily Mail
August, 1998

Broken promises

**Richard Worsley asks why the only type of discrimination
not outlawed is that against the elderly**

It is hard to understand how a political party can make a clear pledge – on the record, through its official spokesperson and ratified by its leader – and then feel able to withdraw its commitment with impunity. And yet this is just what has happened with Labour's pre-election promise to introduce legislation against age discrimination – now the only major cause of discrimination not covered by the law.

It is part of the Government's patchy track record in addressing the needs of people in their third age – the active older members of our population – who should be of major concern to us all. Their numbers are growing, they are of major economic importance and they represent a vital source of wisdom and experience.

On the credit side – apart from the erstwhile commitment on legislation, we have had the welcome launch in June of the Better Government for Older People programme. This is seen as a flagship for 'joined-up government' and is working to achieve improvements in the delivery of services to older people, particularly at local level. And the Government has also announced the creation of an inter-ministerial group charged with developing a co-ordinated strategy on older people.

But it is in the area of employment that Labour's performance has proved particularly disappointing. The pre-election commitment to legislation, so warmly welcomed by all those older people excluded from work simply on grounds of their age, is no longer a commitment. What was once 'we will' is now 'we don't rule it out'.

Having given priority to unemployed younger people in its New Deal, the Government is now turning its attention to those over 25, working through pilot schemes, some of which include provision for unemployed people over 50. But they are addressed only to the registered unemployed and not to the much larger numbers of 'economically inactive' older people – 2.4 million between 50 and retirement age. The reasons why many of these are not claiming unemployment benefits are that they have become so disillusioned and discouraged with their failure to find work that they have given up – or are opting in alarming numbers for sickness benefit.

The pre-election commitment to legislation, so warmly welcomed by all those older people excluded from work simply on grounds of their age, is no longer a commitment

---

Andrew Smith, the minister responsible in these areas, has just published Action On Age – his conclusions from a consultation on age discrimination in employment.

Neither the consultation nor the report have presented an impression of urgency or conviction. There is no explanation of why the commitment to legislation has been abandoned. In a notably partisan section on the subject, all the evidence about the positive role of the law has been ignored – including the report I made to the minister on a recent visit to New Zealand, where there is a view that legislation has had a positive effect.

The centrepiece, as he describes it, of the minister's report is the proposal for a voluntary code of practice, expected shortly – but it seems with no legislative base and no sanctions against employers who disregard it. Yet why should they do otherwise when government itself is giving such a clear message that discrimination on grounds of age warrants less rigorous treatment than all the other major causes of discrimination?

Of course legislation alone is not the answer, but, as Labour made clear in 1996, it is a necessary part of the package needed to persuade employers to mend their ways. Why raise hopes by promising it? Why back away now?

Action on Age is not convincing to real people out there who feel excluded and hopeless, worn down by repeated rejection of their skills and experience because of their age, and who were told that Labour was going to do something very specific about their plight.

Perhaps Mr Smith will yet persuade us not only that he understands their situation but that he will take really effective action to improve it. Three central questions remain unanswered. If there is good reason why 'we will legislate' has turned into 'we might', may we share it? Will he set out some real targets for reducing the extent of age discrimination, monitor performance against them and legislate if they are not met? Will he extend the New Deal not just to the registered unemployed but to all unemployed older people?

Without positive answers to these questions, older voters persuaded by Labour's pre-election promises may feel that they have been taken for a ride.

© *The Guardian*
November, 1998

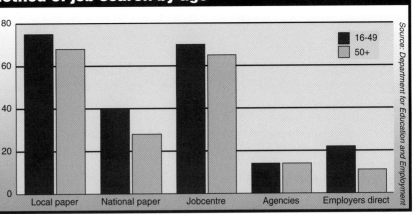

Method of job search by age

When older workers were unemployed and claiming Jobseeker's Allowance, they tended to use fewer methods of job search and look for work less intensively than younger groups. They were, for instance, less likely to use Jobcentre displays or look at the job advertisement sections of national newspapers.

Legend: 16-49, 50+

Categories: Local paper, National paper, Jobcentre, Agencies, Employers direct

Source: Department for Education and Employment

Private lives

You've got qualifications, years of experience – and no job. How do you find work at 50?

The problem

'I am 50, a graduate with a postgraduate qualification. I've worked all my life and earned a reasonable salary, but I was made redundant in 1993 and now find myself in dire poverty and debt. The only reason I can think of is ageism. I've had periods of signing on and doing voluntary work and part-time teaching. I have been told by my local Employment Service that my job search strategy and CV are 'exemplary'. But it's been five years now and I feel powerless and angry, and as if I am in a downward spiral. This is manifesting itself in increasing dependence on prescription drugs and alcohol, loss of confidence, a three-stone increase in weight and poor self-image. The thought of carrying on like this until I'm 60 is humiliating, depressing and frightening. I am also terrified at the prospect of having no pension apart from a state pension. There must be many people in my position. Any suggestions?'

Try temping

Have you tried becoming a temp? If you are desperate for a job and don't mind a career change, you should teach yourself to type, get a couple of books from the library and get yourself on a training course (surely free for long-term unemployed). Go to every employment agency in your area and ask what skills businesses want. Driving? Packing? Computing? A lot of employment agencies will train you in particular 'packages' if you have the basic skills.

I have been a temp for 30 years and have rarely been out of work. I, too, am fat (and over 50) and didn't get the permanent jobs I went for. However, I have been offered permanent posts many times at places where I was temping because I will do anything and I learn fast and work hard. A temporary position will enable you to 'get your foot in the door' and may lead you back into the kind of work you did.

Joan Riley
Stockport

Take charge

There is life after redundancy! I, too, had the big heave, in 1994 when I was in my mid-forties. I, too, thought I would get a job within months. But it didn't work out like that at all; it was only after almost forcing my way into a first interview that I found the problem. My interviewer said: 'You are after my job!' I was a middle manager, I was his age, I was a threat.

I had no option but to go freelance, self-employed, consulting. I have never looked back. If you have a skill people want, they will pay you for it. You don't have the traditional job security, but that's an illusion nowadays. What you do have is control: you are in charge of your business, your career, your life.

Rob Wilson
Cirencester

Let go of your anger

You are almost certainly a victim of ageism and my heart bleeds for you. Society does not value what older and experienced people have to offer.

Your letter demonstrates such courage and clarity and I think you may also be brave enough to take steps to reverse the tide of dependence on drugs, alcohol and food – classic symptoms of low self-esteem. Ask your doctor to help you wean yourself off the drugs, join an

AA group, work out a sensible diet – all these measures will save you money. Learn meditation/relaxation, which will help you manage your situation better. Place reliance in trusted friends. Try to develop an absorbing (and cheap!) hobby. Try to value yourself, in spite of everything. Your anger and frustration are perfectly understandable, but they are only damaging you and draining your emotional resources. Let go of them if you possibly can. Good luck.

Brigid Purcell
Norwich

Rethink your life

We belong to a growing number of fiftysomethings who have to rethink their lives. First, get the word 'redundant' out of your system. We should all be campaigning for a word that doesn't mean 'useless' to replace it. 'Liberated', possibly.

Next, stop thinking everything is out of your control. Your work problems may have been thrust on you by an outside agency but your reactions to them haven't. You don't *have* to drink; you *can* take charge of your weight; you *can* change your priorities in work and spending. All these are your responsibility and no one else's. And you *can* get interested in life again (which will improve your health and self-esteem no end).

You say you do part-time teaching: whether this is in schools or adult education classes, whether it's academic or practical, there's always plenty to do to update your skills. If your classes are lively, informed and fun, the word will get round. And what about all those other things you wanted to discover or do, but never had time for?

No, the state pension doesn't stretch very far, but it's better than nothing and you've earned it. Meanwhile, don't stop looking for ways of earning now. There's always something one hasn't thought of, simply because there was no need to. There is no shame in not having a job, but there may be in letting it beat you.

MM
Norfolk

Be positive

I cannot help but notice that you put your age and qualifications first in your summary of your situation. If you were buying something – a TV, say – would you first want to know about the electronics inside it or would you go for the more aesthetic criteria such as design, image, ease of use? Of course the electronics are critical, but they are not what will sell you the TV.

Look at yourself and identify your selling points. Be positive about your achievements and weave them into a lively and enthusiastic description of yourself. Be positive about your situation. Don't let negative thoughts betray you. Think of a time when you achieved something. I sometimes recall an almost perfect (for me) forehand drive I played one morning on my local tennis court. Recapture the feeling and hold on to it as you write your résumé. Ask yourself: what am I selling? Does anybody want it? If not, what do they want? How can I show it?

Remember, if you keep bashing you head against a brick wall, you will get a headache. Don't waste your time trying the same old things. Do something different. Rip up your CV. It isn't working. Start again, but this time take advice from your local careers adviser who will have a great deal of time for you.

Eddie Costello, Careers adviser
Stockton-on-Tees

Learn new skills

You do not say what you were doing before, but can your difficulty be that you're trying to get back into that type of employment? I was a mature graduate who, at 50, encountered ageism when applying for jobs I felt I was qualified for. I gave up and went back to the secretarial/admin work I'd been doing before I graduated – and I'm still doing it 17 years on. I've found it varied, interesting, at times boring, but better than moping over what might have been. If you do not already have these skills, learn to type, become computer literate, move if feasible to an area where these skills are in demand – and be prepared to start at the bottom.

PN, Guildford

SECRETARIAL INTERVIEWS

Healthy ageing

Information from Helpage International

Ageing is not a disease but a normal part of the life process. Ageing is inevitable and irreversible but does not automatically lead to ill health. Many of the health conditions associated with ageing can be prevented or delayed if people have access to decent living conditions and suitable health care throughout their lives.

For older people who do not receive a pension (the vast majority in the less-developed world), the ability to work and earn a wage is often essential. Good health is a basic requirement if people are to continue to work as they age. A survey in Cambodia in 1998 found that older people identified the inability to work and loss of income as being the most important consequences of illness.

If older people receive health education and have access to medical attention whenever it is necessary, they are less likely to develop serious medical conditions and complications which are more difficult and expensive to treat.

Some health conditions are more likely to occur in older people. Population ageing means that more and more people will reach an age at which there is a higher risk of developing certain chronic, debilitating and disabling conditions. Populations are ageing most rapidly in less-developed countries, where health care systems are generally less well resourced than in the developed world. Policies, systems and structures need to be implemented now to establish healthy ageing programmes and to cope with the pressures ageing populations will place on health services.

Blindness and visual impairment

The likelihood of visual impairment and vision loss increases with age. World-wide, 16 million cases of

blindness are caused by cataracts, which are usually associated with age. In most Asian and African countries cataracts account for more than 50% of all blindness.

Age-related cataract can usually be treated with a simple operation which can be carried out for a low cost in eye clinics or eye camps. Many other age-related visual impairments are also preventable or treatable.

Ageing is not a disease but a normal part of the life process.

Mental health

As populations age, it is likely that there will be an increase in mental health problems. This will happen because people with mental health problems will be living longer and because more people will be living to an age where there is a greater risk of such disorders.

The number of people affected by age-related dementia in Africa, Asia and Latin America is currently estimated at 22 million. By 2025, the number may exceed 80 million. This will mean that the number of people working as informal carers to older people with mental health problems will also increase. Governments, families and communities will all be under pressure to cope with such an increase.

HIV/AIDS

The number of older people with HIV/AIDS is growing. In India 11% of AIDS cases are in people aged 50 or over.

Older people are at risk from HIV in the same way as other people – through sexual activity, the medical use of blood and blood products, and through intravenous drug use. Older people face some particular risks – transfusions of blood and blood products are highest among the older population, and older people may be exposed to body fluids through working as traditional birth attendants and medical practitioners.

In countries where HIV/AIDS is prevalent, older people have often become the principal carers to younger people who have the disease and their children, often also having to take on the role of becoming a family's main breadwinner.

The contribution of older people

Older people often serve their communities as traditional birth attendants and health practitioners. In these capacities they often have positions of respect and are well placed to pass on health education training and messages. Older people are not necessarily a drain on health resources, they are also a potential resource for training and educating their peers and their community in healthy living.

© Helpage International

Home truths

For the first time, a new guide gives invaluable advice on the vexed question of finding a care home for an elderly friend or relative. James Erlichman reports

How many guidebooks are there on child care? Too many to count, and publishers fall over each other to produce the latest, best-selling version. And yet, how many guidebooks are there on old person care? I mean a down-to-earth guide on how to choose a residential or nursing home for an elderly relative or close friend? After all, the responsibility is awesome and the pitfalls are terrifying. The answer: until now, absolutely none.

In fact, the Relatives' Association – a charity which advises families of elderly people – was so desperate it even thought about importing a book on the subject from America, despite the huge differences in the way health and nursing home care is provided.

But yesterday, in the nick of time, a home-grown guide to care homes for the elderly was published, by the King's Fund, a respected British health charity.

What's best about the guide, *Home From Home: Choosing A Care Home*, is that it spares no blushes. It has no truck with weasel words, but dives straight into the home truths of the difficulties to be faced.

First, money. It tells you exactly how much a nursing home is likely to cost a week (£340) versus a residential home (£250) and what the differences are. Next you learn just how poor – in terms of income, property and savings – your loved one will have to be before the state will pick up any of the cost.

But this is a wily guide too. These days, many people live miles from their parents or other elderly relatives. It tells you your local council may be persuaded to help find a home for your relative if they are willing to move to be near you. But it warns that local authorities are not required to hand over the inspection reports that they are obliged to make on care homes in their areas.

It is wily, but above all, chock full of useful information. Councils must provide a 'care manager' responsible for devising the 'care plan' for the elderly person. This can be very detailed. Can your loved one come on a trial period? Is their room guaranteed to be theirs, or can they be forced to move? Can they bring their own furniture, including a TV? Above all, the guide is practical, telling you literally to follow your nose by inhaling the home as soon as you walk in – getting a good whiff of its smell will tell you a lot straight away.

> ### What's best about the guide is that it dives straight into the home truths of the difficulties to be faced

---

It gets even better. Don't forget to ask whether residents can smoke or drink on the premises, and if so, whether incontinence pads are provided. Alas, the guide doesn't tell you to ask whether boy or girl friends can share their beds occasionally for the night, but I genuinely hope the authors discreetly provide this advice in the next edition.

Above all, the guide warns that you are unlikely to find the perfect

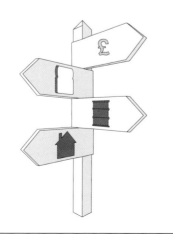

home for your elderly relative. Trying to assess someone else's needs and tastes are bad enough. But finding the perfect home with, say, excellent gardens, spacious rooms with a view, an excellent menu, a liberal policy about activities and friends, coupled with first-class nursing and other medical care when needed, is virtually impossible. It tells you to fight for your rights every inch of the way, but warns that some compromises from both you and the would-be resident are almost inevitable and should not be the source of your subsequent guilt when the home you choose reveals its shortcomings.

Of course, all prototypes have their shortcomings – and since this is the first comprehensive guide to care homes in Britain, *Home From Home* is not without its faults. Jef Smith is general manager of Counsel and Care, a charity which gives advice and help to older people who are pondering whether to go into a home. He also sits on a government working party helping to draft a new law to set minimum national standards in care homes.

'It's a very good effort and there is a lot to praise about *Home From Home*,' he says. 'But my main criticism is that at more than 70 pages it may be too detailed for many older people. And there doesn't seem any real hierarchy to the questions it poses – it needs to prioritise more.' For example, Jef Smith's top tip on choosing a home is: 'Take a deep sniff the second you walk in. If you smell urine, walk straight out again.' The advice in the guide on using your nose is somewhat buried on page 45.

• To obtain a copy of *Home From Home: Choosing A Care Home* (£5.95), published by the King's Fund, telephone the King's Fund Bookshop on 0171 307 2591.

© *The Guardian*
October, 1998

Town halls 'still plundering the elderly in care'

Old people in care homes are still being routinely fleeced by town halls, a charity said yesterday. They are being made to pay their own bills even though the law says they should be allowed to keep some of their savings for themselves, according to Help the Aged.

The allegation follows months of unease about the unwillingness of councils to stick to government rules on which old people they should and should not help. Local authorities have repeatedly challenged the law which says an old person should have help with care home bills after his or her savings drop below £16,000 and that the whole bill should be paid when there is only £10,000 left.

A landmark court case last year stopped one left-wing council, Sefton on Merseyside, insisting that the elderly paid their own bills until all they had was the price of their own funeral – £1,500.

Help the Aged said yesterday that it knew of 2,000 cases where elderly home residents had been forced to pay their own bills even though they had less than the savings threshold.

By Steve Doughty, Social Affairs Correspondent

Its policy adviser Gail Elkington said: 'Councils cannot go on blatantly ignoring the law. The poor treatment of older people at a very difficult time in their lives is entirely unacceptable – we must find a way of forcing councils to abide by the law.'

> **'Councils cannot go on blatantly ignoring the law. The poor treatment of older people at a very difficult time in their lives is entirely unacceptable'**

Authorities, she said, were pleading poverty and refusing to pay for care, or alternatively delaying payment.

The charity cited one case in which an elderly woman had been forced to pay her own care home fees despite having under £16,000 because the council had 'no money in the budget' to meet its obligations. In another case, a woman had been left in hospital for nine months because a council refused to pay for a place in a home.

The argument over who pays for care has been growing in political impact over the last few years as councils try to avoid handing over Care in the Community money given them by the Department of Health.

Families are regularly shaken by the discovery that councils can force couples to sell their homes – depriving children of their inheritance – to meet bills which average £250 a week.

Help the Aged said it had received allegations that councils had improperly tried to avoid paying their bills in Liverpool, Sefton, Dorset, Cambridgeshire, Manchester, Bury, Harrow, Hertfordshire, Bromley, Cheshire, Cumbria, Surrey, Gloucestershire, Essex, Mid Glamorgan, Berkshire, Hereford and Worcester, West Sussex, and Sheffield.

© *The Daily Mail*
July, 1998

When older people need care . . .

Older people are often perceived as being frail and in need of extensive care. Because of this, there is much emphasis on the burden this lays on families, communities and governments.

Many older people, particularly the 'oldest old', do need care, but many remain independent and economically active well into extreme old age.

Very often older people can, and wish to, continue to contribute to their communities even when they are no longer able to be fully independent.

Most care of older people is provided by informal and community structures. In England in 1992, only 4% of people over 65 were living in residential homes and nursing homes.

Care is economic sense

If older people who need care are able to receive it, their quality of life is maintained and they are more able to contribute to their families and communities. Adequate care when it is necessary can prevent many health problems, reducing the risk of disability and the need for expensive medical and hospital treatment.

The increasing need for care

The sector of the older population most likely to require care is the 'oldest old'. In many countries, particularly in the less-developed world, this is the fastest-growing group in the older population. This means that there is an increasing need for care.

In many countries the number of older people with disabilities – who may need increasing support as they age – is also growing rapidly.

Care in the family

There is a general belief that older people in less-developed countries automatically receive care and protection from their extended family.

There is evidence which suggests that, particularly in countries where there are few social services, the responsibility of caring for frail older people is indeed often taken on by the family. However, in many places the traditional family structure is changing – because of economic forces, migration, HIV/AIDS, or increasing poverty – and this is affecting people's ability to provide for their older relatives.

Rapid urbanisation is also causing these patterns of care to change.

Generally speaking, older people are becoming less able to rely on their families for support.

Caring for each other

In many places older people have developed strategies for caring for themselves and each other. In this way they receive and give care and support, remain independent and have control over their own lives.

- In Sri Lanka each older person attending a day centre in a small community has adopted another older person in the village who is housebound, sharing their time, food and finances and assisting them with daily tasks.
- In Bolivia a group of very poor older women have worked together to live and work in their own self-supporting environment. They have built their own house and created an income-generating programme; they provide food for themselves and others and are well respected in their community.
- In Cambodia a small group of older people live together in a building within the grounds of a temple. Other older people gather there in the day time. The older people support each other, provide social services to people of all ages within their community, and hold religious services. In return their community donates money and food to the group.

When older people are the carers

Many older people – particularly women – are themselves caring for others.

These may be:

- Other older people – spouse, partner, family members
- Children whose parents are working, have died or are unable to care for them
- Their own adult children who are sick – this happens particularly in countries where HIV/AIDS is widespread.

In taking on the responsibility of care, older people all over the world are freeing other people to undertake paid work. In this way they are actively contributing to economic development, even if they are not wage-earners themselves.

Care at home

Very often older people, wherever they are, prefer to remain in their own homes as long as possible. This

---

Many older people, do need care, but many remain independent and economically active well into extreme old age

---

can be achieved with the help of family, friends, neighbours, community and formal and informal social services (assistance with daily tasks, transport, others in the community providing a daily meal, home visiting programmes, community social and health services).

Abuse and neglect

When older people are frail or dependent on others for their daily

needs, they may be vulnerable to abuse or neglect. Safeguards to protect physically or mentally frail older people, as well as support and training for their carers, are issues which urgently need addressing in an ageing world.

Caring for the carers

Caring for older people can be a stressful activity, especially if the person is dependent, very ill, or has dementia. People who are caring need the support of others in their family and community and organisations working with older people.

- The above is an extract from Helpage International's web site which can be found at http://www.oneworld.org/helpage

© Helpage International

Old people's homes 'hide the true cost'

Old people's homes were accused yesterday of giving many residents a raw deal.

They fail to reveal their true charges and hide important financial information in small print, the Office of Fair Trading said.

Residents were often afraid to complain, its report added, while there was a 'potential for conflict' over the managing of residents' money.

The survey of 965 residents in homes in England, Scotland and Wales, follows a *Daily Mail* campaign which highlighted the way families can spend their inheritance paying for care home places.

It also revealed how social workers and hospitals shunt the elderly into residential care rather than make efforts to help them live with their families.

The OFT report said brochures for old people's homes often fail to provide adequate information about fees and what they include. Among those surveyed, only one mentioned extra charges for hairdressing, chiropody and outings.

Only one resident in ten moving

By Steve Doughty, Social Affairs Correspondent

---

into a council-run home was given written information beforehand in the form of a leaflet or brochure.

Those moving into privately-run homes fared little better, the report said.

Four residents in five either did not know of any written contract concerning their care or were unaware of its contents.

Key conditions – including potentially costly clauses governing the termination of a contract – were 'missing or hidden within small print or unnecessarily legalistic language'.

Three-quarters of residents surveyed said they were satisfied with their care but 'even when residents

---

'In an ideal world, people would have clear and accurate information'

---

were aware of how to complain, they were reluctant to do so for fear of alienating staff or victimisation'.

John Bridgeman, the Director General of Fair Trading, said: 'The inquiry confirms fears that vital information is not reaching those who need it when they need it most. It is essential that older consumers get the best possible deal.

'In an ideal world, people would have clear and accurate information to enable them to shop around to find the care home most suited to their needs.

'In fact decisions are often made in a hurry, particularly when a patient is being transferred from hospital.'

The OFT is preparing guidelines to cover residential and nursing homes, which care for more than 500,000 people.

It says inspectors should be given powers to monitor the handling of residents' finances.

The report comes as a Royal Commission continues to take evidence about the long-term care of the elderly.

© The Daily Mail
October, 1998

The 'invisible' patients

Elderly face neglect and misery in NHS hospitals says charity

Older patients are routinely neglected by the National Health Service, campaigners claim today.

They are given poor quality care and receive no support at home once they have been discharged, it is alleged.

Their needs are often the last to be met because the health service is under pressure, according to Help the Aged. The charity says almost half of hospital patients are 60 or over, but frequently become 'invisible' within the NHS – where they are left for hours on trolleys and then dumped in dirty wards.

Help the Aged is launching Dignity on the Ward, a campaign to improve hospital care and combat age discrimination.

Campaign leader Dr Simon Festing said the recent beds crisis triggered by the flu outbreak is an everyday reality for thousands of the elderly.

'For too many older people, a stay in hospital is a nightmare experience,' he added. 'Older people's needs are often the last to be met on overstretched wards, despite many doctors and nurses working to provide the best service they can.'

A survey by the charity found 'shocking levels of ill-treatment', he said. 'One patient described his stay in hospital as being like torture. Patients are not given enough attention, especially by front-line staff such as nurses, although many older people recognised the pressure under which staff were working.'

Among complaints listed were delays in admission, including waiting on trolleys; dirty wards; insufficient food and no help with feeding; mixed wards, communal toilet and bathroom facilities; poor communication between staff, and between hospitals, GPs and social workers; and poorly planned discharges with no home-care support.

By Jenny Hope and Terri Judd

Dr Festing said lack of respect is the most frequent complaint.

'Many older people don't like being called by their Christian names, but their wishes are ignored,' he added. 'They don't want to be on mixed wards where they're afraid to ask for a commode and embarrassed by badly-fitting gowns, but they often don't get a choice.'

Help the Aged wants more trained staff on wards, a review of the NHS complaints procedure to produce rapid changes for patients, and better planning of hospital discharge.

The charity's survey follows a report by Health Advisory Service 2000, an independent body of medical researchers, which condemned unacceptably long waits in admission, wards in poor repair, and shortage of equipment and basic supplies.

Staff did not always assist patients who needed help with eating, food and drink was often of poor quality and there were problems with preserving patients' privacy and dignity.

> *'For too many older people, a stay in hospital is a nightmare experience,' he added. 'Older people's needs are often the last to be met on overstretched wards'*

'Conditions were disgusting'

Maureen Oakley, 61, went into hospital for a hip replacement and left with a broken breastbone.

'I suffer from rheumatoid arthritis and went into the William Harvey Hospital in Ashford for a hip replacement,' said Mrs Oakley, of Hawkinge, Kent. 'There were supposed to be two nurses helping me in and out of bed, but because of a shortage they could only find one. On the fifth night, I fell and broke a bone in my chest.'

Matters became progressively worse when she was transferred nearer home to the Royal Victoria Hospital, Folkestone.

'I was in a ward for 12 and the toilets were absolutely disgusting,' she said. 'At one point, I was in the middle of washing and the nurses left me. Some other girl had to take over. It was a terrible experience.'

'I couldn't get any information'

Diane Kelly was appalled at the lack of care for her father at Stafford District General. Having already suffered a stroke and heart attack, Patrick Jocelyn, 73, had to be admitted two weeks ago with pneumonia.

Mrs Kelly said her family failed to get any information from staff, who had lost his notes. She was horrified to find last Monday that no one was supervising his medication or meals. 'He is very confused. I found his tablets at the bottom of his cup. You can't expect him to take them on his own, the same with his food.

'I couldn't get any information from the nurses. They were too busy on the phone, eating crisps and feeding each other liquorice allsorts. They ignored us.

'My father is allergic to penicillin. They couldn't find his notes. I know some nurses work hard but this lot were mucking about.'

© *The Daily Mail
January, 1999*

Family break-ups 'spell disaster for care of the elderly'

By Steve Doughty, Social Affairs Correspondent

The breakdown of the traditional family may prove disastrous for the future care of the elderly, it was claimed yesterday.

There is a danger that the rising divorce rate could 'blur lines of obligation between parents and children' and affect the way families care for old people, according to a study.

Government-sponsored researchers found that despite the growing numbers of elderly who need long-term care, few people are keen to pay for it.

The survey, carried out by academics at Leicester University, comes in the wake of hints by ministers – and prompted by a *Daily Mail* campaign – that they are considering tax breaks for carers to encourage more families to look after their own frail elderly members.

The impact of the erosion of the traditional family led by a married husband and wife on elderly people has yet to be explored in depth by analysts.

Professor Gillian Parker, of the Nuffield Community Care Studies Unit at Leicester, suggests the growth of single-parent families, cohabitation, and divorce is likely to have a major impact on the increasing numbers of older people who will have to be cared for in the next century.

Her research found that most people believed the Government should play a major role in caring for the old. Many accepted there should be personal responsibility – but were not clear on who should pay.

Two-thirds were unhappy with the current means-tested system of providing state support for old people in residential homes.

The system means that anyone with more than £10,000 in savings will have to pay towards their own bills – and councils can make elderly people sell their homes to meet care costs.

Few of the 950 people polled were prepared to use the value of their home to pay for a place in a home, the study found.

It is the decline of the family that is one of the biggest concerns

'There is the sense of betrayal for those who thought that they were buying a home which they could pass on to their children, only to find that they are asked to sell it to pay for their own care,' said Professor Parker.

The survey, called *Who Will Pay for Long-Term Care?* and financed by the Economic and Social Research Council, found only 6 per cent of people willing to take insurance to pay for care late in life.

'That is not an irrational attitude,' said Professor Parker. 'These are very long-term risks which are hard to predict – you can worry now about your car being stolen but whether you will need care when you are 80 is a difficult thing to think about insuring for.'

The Tory government's 'partnership' idea – in which the state would allow people to keep their savings if they met part of the cost of their care from insurance – brought support from only half those quizzed.

Professor Parker warns: 'The number of older people is rising just at a time when the number of traditional carers – women who stay at home and are not in paid employment – is falling.

'This latest research shows that although political thinking about who should pay for care in old age has radically changed over the last 20 years, the public's attitude and behaviour have not.'

However, it is the decline of the family that is one of the biggest concerns.

Professor Parker added: 'The family has been the traditional provider of care for most older people, particularly through the unpaid work of women, although state and private services also play an important role, particularly for those who live alone.

...DO YOU HAVE A FAMILY?

...I'M NOT SURE THESE DAYS...

'Changing family size and structure, women's increased labour market participation, and the possibility of blurred lines of obligation between parents and children as a result of rising rates of divorce and remarriage may all affect this traditional source of care.'

She said a national debate on how to pay for the care of old people was 'overdue'.

A Royal Commission on caring for the elderly – likely to be launched by Health Minister Paul Boateng in the near future – will consider the new findings.

Warning to Brown on 'tax trap'

Experts warned yesterday that one of Gordon Brown's most ambitious welfare proposals would do nothing to improve family life.

They declared that integrating the tax and benefit system – as the Chancellor dreams of doing – could be a mistake.

Giving evidence to the Commons Social Security Select Committee, the specialists also said the current system was biased against families and in favour of single mothers.

Mr Brown wants to merge the tax and benefit system as part of his crusade to destroy the poverty traps

---

Despite the growing numbers of elderly who need long-term care, few people are keen to pay for it

---

that discourage people from seeking work. Barclays chief executive Martin Taylor has been appointed to head a task force which will study the 'streamlining' of the two systems.

The Chancellor has specifically asked him to consider the virtues of American-style earned income tax credits, a form of 'negative income tax' to replace benefits for low earners.

Announcing the task force, the Treasury said it would produce plans to 'strengthen community and family life'.

But yesterday MPs were told that integrating taxes and benefits posed many problems.

Paul Johnson, deputy director of the Institute of Fiscal Studies, said the potential advantages were 'very difficult to quantify', yet there would be 'significant' disadvantages,

particularly because the tax system related to individual earnings and the benefit system to household earnings.

Pamela Meadows, director of the Policy Studies Institute, commented: 'It is probable that the administration of the new system would be more complex than the one we have currently, and that this may mean greater financial risks to families with incomes on the margins.'

Patricia Morgan, another social policy expert giving evidence to the committee's inquiry into the tax and benefits system, complained that the system did not take enough account of the fact that 'some people have family responsibilities and some do not'.

A campaign to persuade the Chancellor to make the tax system fairer for families is being launched today by the Christian Action, Research and Education pressure group.

It wants Tony Blair to honour the promise he made at the Labour conference to put support for the family at the heart of Government policy.

The group says the tax burden on families has more than doubled over the last 30 years.

© *The Daily Mail*

Elder abuse

Information from Action on Elder Abuse

What is elder abuse?

Elder abuse is defined by Action on Elder Abuse as:

A single or repeated act or lack of appropriate action, occurring within any relationship where there is an expectation of trust, which causes harm or distress to an older person.

There are five main types of abuse:

- physical – for example, hitting, slapping, burning, pushing, restraining or giving too much medication or the wrong medication;

- psychological – for example, shouting, swearing, frightening, blaming, ignoring or humiliating a person;
- financial – for example, the illegal or unauthorised use of a person's property, money, pension book or other valuables;
- sexual – for example, forcing a person to take part in any sexual activity without his or her consent – this can occur in any relationship;
- neglect – for example, where a person is deprived of food, heat, clothing or comfort or essential medication.

An older person may either suffer from only one form of abuse, or different types of abuse at the same time.

Who abuses?

- A partner, child or relative.
- A friend or neighbour.
- A volunteer worker
- A health, social care or other worker.

Where does abuse occur?

Abuse can occur in an individual's own home, in a carer's home, in a day centre, in a residential or nursing home or in a hospital.

Why does it happen?

Abuse occurs for many reasons and the causes are not fully understood. The following risk factors have been identified as being associated with physical and psychological abuse (one or more may be present in any abusive situation):

- social isolation – as those who are abused usually have fewer social contacts than those who are not abused;
- there is a history of a poor quality long-term relationship between the abused and the abuser;
- a pattern of family violence exists. The person who abuses may have been abused as a child;
- the person who abuses is dependent upon the person they abuse for accommodation, financial and emotional support;
- the person who abuses has a history of mental health problems or a personality disorder or a drug or alcohol problem

In care settings abuse may be a symptom of a poorly run establishment. It appears that it is most likely to occur when staff are inadequately trained, poorly supervised, have little support from management or work in isolation.

Prevalence of abuse

In 1992 a UK national prevalence study by Ogg and Bennett was published. This showed that up to 5% of older people in the community were suffering from verbal abuse and up to 2% were the victims of physical or financial abuse.

There have been no prevalence studies undertaken in the UK on abuse in care settings.

The law and elder abuse

There are two relevant strands of law – prevention and protection.

Protection is available through the criminal and civil courts, both to prevent a person being abused and to take action against the abuser.

However comparatively little use has been made of the law and many people may be unwilling to undertake legal proceedings. Consultation with an appropriately trained and qualified legal adviser is strongly advised when considering using the law. The preventative statutes are the Health Services and Public Health Act 1968 which allows local authorities to promote the welfare of older people and the NHS and Community Care Act 1990 which requires them to undertake an assessment of need. Sections of the Mental Health Act 1983 may be used where the older person is mentally ill and believed to be ill-treated or neglected.

Under Section 47 of the National Assistance Act 1948 a local authority has the power to seek an order from a magistrate's court authorising the removal from their home of a person at severe risk. The application must be supported by a certificate from a community physician that the person is either:

- suffering from a grave and chronic disease; or
- is aged, infirm or physically incapacitated and living in unsanitary conditions and is unable to look after him or herself and is not receiving proper care and attention from others.

Seeking an order for removal should be a last resort after all other options have been tried.

Criminal actions can be brought against the physical abuser using the Offences Against the Person Act 1861. The Domestic Violence and Matrimonial Proceedings Act and the Sexual Offences Act can also be used in certain circumstances.

Legislation on domestic violence, including the Family Law Act 1996, may be used against a wide range of abusers who live with the abused person. It is not confined to spouses.

Arrangements can be made for the Court of Protection to manage the financial affairs of someone who is mentally incapable.

A power of attorney, enduring power of attorney and the appointee system of the Department of Social Security may be helpful in some instances of financial abuse.

• The above is information from Action on Elder Abuse. See page 41 for address details.

© Action on Elder Abuse

Mental illness

Mental health and older people

The purpose of this article is to inform older people, their friends and relatives, about some of the mental health problems that can occur in old age.

One of the greatest success stories of this century has been the extension of life expectancy. During the past few decades, the size and age structure of the United Kingdom's population has changed dramatically. One-fifth of the total population is now aged over 60 compared with 7.5 per cent at the beginning of the century. In 1991 there were 7.62 million people aged 65 and over in England of whom 765,000 were aged 85 and over.

What this means is that many people can now anticipate a substantial period following retirement in which they can actively pursue leisure activities and hobbies free from the worries of work or children.

Older people can enjoy life and have just as much fun in later years as at any other time. Staying reasonably fit will make it possible to get the maximum enjoyment out of life. One of the bars to enjoying life, however, can be the presence of problems with physical or mental health.

Mental illness is treatable

Just like physical illness, mental illness covers a wide range of symptoms. When older, bereavement, ill health or loneliness can contribute to its development. Mental illness is also similar to physical illness in that a wide range of treatments is available. It is a myth that treatment becomes more difficult as you get older. Modern research and medical experience have confirmed that treatment works regardless of age.

The most common mental health problems in old age are anxiety and difficulty in sleeping. Most older people retain full control of their faculties as they age. Only six per cent of people aged over 65 suffer from dementia. Dementia is the general term for memory loss and confusion, the most common cause being Alzheimer's disease.

Sleep problems

Most adults require between seven and eight hours' sleep each night. It is said that older people need less sleep but in fact they may just have different sleeping patterns.

As people age they are more likely to need to get up during the night to go to the lavatory, disturbing their normal sleep pattern. Painfully immobilising conditions such as arthritis or Parkinson's disease may also contribute to sleeping problems. Drinking coffee, tea or alcohol late at night may make this kind of problem worse.

Disturbed and fragmented sleep

Sleeping tablets do not necessarily help and are not recommended for long-term use. They can cause drowsiness the following day and may cause side-effects such as poor memory and giddiness. They are also just as addictive in older people as in younger people. An alternative to sleeping tablets is to keep physically active and involved with other people; it is not a good idea to sleep during the day and food and drink should be taken early in the evening.

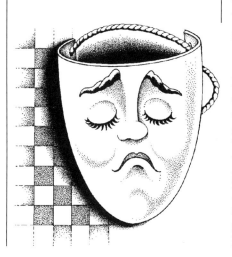

If none of these approaches to healthy sleeping works, then it is important that you consult your doctor to ensure that lack of sleep is not caused by physical and mental health problems.

Depression and physical health

Certain physical illnesses may trigger unhappiness and frustration. Arthritis is the most common cause of long-standing illness in old age and can be a major cause of sadness and depression. Pain, particularly in the knee, hip, shoulders, neck and back, may make it difficult to carry out ordinary but essential tasks such as shopping, cooking or personal care such as cutting toenails.

Experts are becoming increasingly aware that treating arthritis can dramatically improve quality of life for sufferers. A mixture of painkillers and physiotherapy can reduce the pain and restore some independence.

Lack of physical activity and being overweight can make arthritis much worse. Although many people who suffer from this condition want to retreat into the safety of their own home, it is far better to join in activities and get stiff joints moving again.

Similar problems can be faced by people suffering from Parkinson's disease or heart disease. Again, treatments are available and it is far better to participate in activities rather than avoid them.

Depression

Between 11 per cent and 14 per cent of older people suffer from symptoms of depression, although only about one to two per cent are considered to be severely affected. Depression can be made worse by poor physical health, the lack of a close friend, loneliness and widowhood as well as recent deaths and accidents amongst near relatives or friends. Other major life events such as moving house, moving into residential care, acute illness, and separation can all lead to the development of a depressive illness.

I am not depressed but I often cry with frustration and have major problems sleeping

Everybody gets miserable from time to time, that's no surprise. But normally we all find ways of getting over it. When there's a depressive disorder, however, the sufferer may have a feeling of great sadness which never goes away. There may also be a lack of interest in life, tiredness and fatigue, as well as a loss of appetite and weight.

People with this condition start to withdraw from company and experience difficulties with sleeping. Sufferers may then begin to lose their confidence, start to feel bad about current or past events, and occasionally even harbour suicidal thoughts.

Some people with depression have symptoms they think are caused by physical disease but in fact are caused by the depression itself. Concern about their physical symptoms may make them appear anxious, worried and/or confused. They may feel that they are becoming a burden to their family and wish that they could pull themselves together. It may even be an effort to do the simplest task, such as making a cup of tea or getting dressed.

Obviously, the first port of call must be the doctor who should be able to make a diagnosis of depression from the symptoms and signs. He or she will then recommend a course of treatment or further sources of help.

Dementia

Alzheimer's disease is the most common form of the group of disorders known as the dementias. Dementia means a progressive decline in the ability to remember, think and reason. Although it occurs more often in older people, younger people are sometimes – although rarely – affected. Dementia can cause a progressive loss of memory, language and communication, eventually leading to an inability to feed or dress, incontinence and eventually, death.

Alzheimer's disease is responsible for about half of all cases of dementia. The next most common type is multi-infarct dementia. In this case, a series of small strokes creates a number of dead regions in the brain. Each stroke may be so small that the sufferer is not even aware that anything has happened.

Other possible causes of dementia are Parkinson's disease, Pick's disease, Huntington's disease and some people with AIDS are also at risk. However, not everybody with these diseases develops dementia.

Who does dementia affect?

More than half a million people in the UK suffer from some form of dementia:

- 20 per cent over the age of 80 are affected
- 6 per cent aged over 65 are affected.

Common problems in dementia

The first sign of dementia is usually an inability to remember recent events and names. People with mild dementia may become uninterested in hobbies and activities, apathetic, have problems adapting to change and appear frightened of trying new things. Because they are slower at grasping complex ideas, they have difficulty making decisions or plans.

People with moderate dementia may become disorientated regarding time and place, as well as fail to remember recent events. This inability may cause them to become very dependent, particularly when not in their familiar surroundings, and also to forget the names of friends and family.

With severe dementia, the sufferer is very disabled and requires a great deal of help and support. Their symptoms will have progressed to a state where he or she may not be able to find their way around, cannot remember for even a few minutes whether they have eaten, and will constantly repeat one or more phrases.

One common problem is wandering around or away from home. Communication can become increasingly difficult as dementia progresses, causing problems for both sufferers and relatives.

If incontinence becomes a problem, it can seem like the last straw for a carer or someone with dementia. But there are measures that can be taken to alleviate the problem or make it less stressful. Advice can be obtained from a local health service continence adviser.

Sometimes the person with dementia may behave in a very aggressive manner. Aggression often arises from the person's fears and confusion and is not intended. Such behaviour may make carers feel shocked and distressed, but your local Departments of Health and Social Services offer help with these kinds of problems.

It should be mentioned that people do not necessarily progress from mild dementia to more severe forms. Once the diagnosis has been

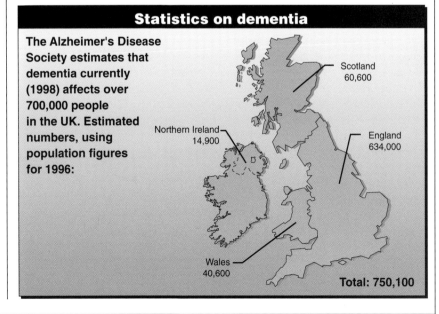

Statistics on dementia

The Alzheimer's Disease Society estimates that dementia currently (1998) affects over 700,000 people in the UK. Estimated numbers, using population figures for 1996:

Scotland 60,600

Northern Ireland 14,900

England 634,000

Wales 40,600

Total: 750,100

made, it is impossible to predict exactly how people will respond to treatment. With adequate support, individuals and their carers can still have a good quality of life. Older people with varying degrees of dementia can all benefit from a consultation with a general practitioner and, when necessary, a specialist.

Carers

Carers who may themselves be elderly and/or disabled often look after elderly relatives in distressing circumstances. This responsibility, coupled perhaps with the stress of trying to hold down a job at the same time, can mean that their physical and mental health suffer. Feelings of loneliness and despair are common as well as depression, especially if the relative, who may be their life-long partner, no longer recognises them or is aggressive towards them. This, in association with poor or disturbed sleep, can lead to tiredness or exhaustion.

Respite care

It is important that carers look after themselves as well as ensure that their relative is well cared for. Carers may need to take a break once in a while, by arranging for the relative either to attend day care sessions or to stay in some form of residential accommodation for a while. Respite care of this kind should be discussed with social services or with the GP, district nurse or health visitor. There are other forms of respite care, such as the home care service which may be able to help a carer with daily caring tasks, and sitting services which provide relief for the carer in the home. The National Carers' Association can offer general support and advice.

Depression
Most people with depression can be successfully treated by their GP. In some cases, the GP may enlist the support of a specialist old age psychiatrist who will make an initial assessment in the person's home. Treatment for depression is the same for older people as for younger people.

Dementia/Alzheimer's disease
Although Alzheimer's disease is not curable at the moment, there are other conditions that at first sight appear similar for which effective treatments are available. There is no simple straightforward test for Alzheimer's disease. Diagnosis is made by excluding other possible causes of memory loss or confusion. In most cases, a diagnosis will emerge from a home visit made by the family doctor and a specialist. It is important for relatives to ask that the sufferer be medically examined. A number of medical investigations should be initiated to see whether any of these treatable conditions is present. The family doctor will usually ask a hospital specialist to help in this task of ruling out other conditions.

Medicines for Alzheimer's disease
A number of medicines that may help reduce some of the symptoms of Alzheimer's disease are being developed and may be available in the next few years. These are likely to benefit a small proportion of people with Alzheimer's disease and then usually in the earliest stages.

- The above information is from *Mental Illness – Mental health and older people*, produced by Health of the Nation, Department of Health.

Understanding and respecting the person with dementia

Information from the Alzheimer's Disease Society

If you are caring for someone with dementia you will want to ensure that they are always treated with respect and dignity and as an individual person, however little they may seem to understand.

Someone with dementia, whose mental abilities are declining, will feel vulnerable and in need of reassurance and support. It is important that those around them do everything they can to help them retain their sense of identity and their feelings of worth. They will need to remember that:
- Each person with dementia is a unique individual with their own very different experiences of life, their own needs and feelings and their own likes and dislikes.
- Each person will be affected by their dementia in a different way.

Those caring for people with dementia will need to take account of their abilities, interests and preferences as they are at present, and the fact that these may change as the dementia progresses. They should be prepared to respond in a flexible and sensitive way.

Background information
The more background information you can give about the person's past, as well as their present situation, the easier it will be for others to see them as a whole person rather than simply as someone with dementia. They may then feel more confident about finding topics of conversation or suggesting activities that the person may enjoy.

You may need to remind others that:
- Dementia is nothing to be ashamed of and that it is no one's fault.
- Dementia may cause the person to behave in ways that others find irritating or upsetting but that this is not deliberate.

- People with dementia often remember the past far more clearly than the recent present and are often happy to talk about their memories, unless these are painful.

The right name

Our sense of who we are is closely connected to the name or names we are known by. It is important to make sure that others address the person with dementia in a way they recognise and prefer.

- Some people may be happy for anyone to call them by their first name or the name used by friends and family.
- Others may prefer younger people or those who do not know them well to use a courtesy title such as 'Mr' or 'Mrs'.

You may come from a cultural background which has its own particular way of using names and of addressing people in order to show respect. If so, make sure you explain this clearly to anyone from a different background who is in contact with the person with dementia so that they can use the appropriate name or courtesy title.

Culture and religion

Make sure that anyone caring for the person, however briefly, has appropriate details about any relevant cultural or religious customs or beliefs so that these can be respected. These may range from diet, clothing and the use of jewellery, for example, to ways of undressing, doing hair, washing or toileting. Some forms of touch which are taken for granted in some cultures may be thought disrespectful in others. You may need to explain any religious observances such as prayer and festivals as well as other traditions.

Treating as an adult

It is important that everyone continues to treat the person as an adult and with courtesy, however advanced their dementia.

- Be kind and reassuring without talking down to them as though they were a small child.
- Never talk over their heads as though they weren't there.
- Do not talk about the person in

front of them unless they are included in the conversation.
- Avoid scolding or criticising the person as this will make them feel small.
- Look for the meaning behind what they may be trying to communicate, even if it does not seem on the surface to make sense.

Focus on abilities

Help the person avoid situations in which they are bound to fail since this can be humiliating. Look for tasks they can still manage and activities they can still enjoy.

- Give them plenty of praise and encouragement and let them do things at their own pace and in their own way.
- Do things with the person, rather than for them, so they can preserve some independence.
- Break activities down into small steps so that the person has some feeling of achievement, even if they can only manage part of a task.
- Much of our self-respect is often bound up in the way we look. Encourage the person to take a pride in their appearance and give them plenty of praise.

Respecting privacy

Try to make sure that the person's right to privacy is respected.
- You may suggest that people

knock on their bedroom door before entering, for example.
- If the person needs help with intimate activities such as washing or going to the toilet this should be done in a sensitive way. Make sure the bathroom door is kept closed if other people are around.

Offering choice

It is important that the person with dementia should be informed and wherever possible consulted about matters which concern them. They should also be given every opportunity to make appropriate choices.

- Even if you are unsure how much they can understand, always explain what you are doing and why. You may then be able to judge their reaction from their expression or body language.
- Although too many choices can be confusing, you can continue to offer choice by phrasing questions that only need a yes or no answer such as, 'Would you like to wear your blue jumper today?'

Expressing feelings

People with dementia are likely to be sad or upset at times. They have the right to expect those caring for them to try and understand how they feel and to make time to offer support rather than ignoring them or jollying them along.

In the earlier stages people may want to talk about their anxieties and the problems they are experiencing. It is important that others do not brush these worries aside, however painful they may be, but listen and show that they are there for them.

Feeling valued

The person with dementia needs to feel respected and valued for who they are now, as well as for who they were in the past. It helps if those caring:

- are flexible and tolerant
- can make time to listen and to chat and enjoy being with the person
- can show affection as appropriate.

© Alzheimer's Disease Society
October, 1997

What is Alzheimer's disease?

Information from the Alzheimer's Disease Society

Alzheimer's disease is the most common cause of dementia, responsible for just over half of the 670,000 cases in the UK. This article describes symptoms and the likely course of the disease, as well as diagnosis and prospects for treatment.

Symptoms

Typically Alzheimer's disease begins with lapses of memory, difficulty in finding the right words for everyday objects or mood swings. Mild symptoms may be a natural effect of ageing, but in Alzheimer's disease a pattern of problems emerges over six months or more.

As it progresses the person may:
- routinely forget recent events, appointments, names and faces and have difficulty in understanding what is being said.
- become confused when handling money, driving a car or using a washing machine.
- undergo personality changes, appearing no longer to care about those around them, and becoming irritable or apathetic.
- suffer mood swings and burst into tears for no apparent reason, or become convinced that someone is trying to harm them.

In advanced cases people may also:
- adopt unsettling behaviour, like getting up in the middle of the night, or wandering off from their home and becoming lost.
- lose their inhibitions and sense of suitable behaviour, undressing in public or making inappropriate sexual advances.

Finally, the personality disintegrates and the person becomes totally dependent or bed-bound. Relatives have described this experience as like living with a stranger.

What causes these symptoms?

Alzheimer's is a physical disease which attacks brain cells (where we store memory) and brain nerves and transmitters (which carry instructions around the brain). Production of a chemical messenger acetylcholine is disrupted, nerve ends are attacked and cells die. The brain shrinks as gaps develop in the temporal lobe and hippo-campus, important for receiving and storing new information. The ability to remember, speak, think and make decisions is disrupted. After death, tangles and plaques made from protein fragments, dying cells and nerve ends are discovered in the brain. This confirms the diagnosis.

What causes Alzheimer's disease?

The short answer is we don't know. It may be a combination of factors, some we are born with, some in our environment and some which happen to us. Things that make Alzheimer's disease more likely are called 'risk factors'. They include:

Age
The greatest risk factor is increasing age.
- Below the age of 65 dementia affects one person in 1,000.
- Over the age of 65 it affects four to five in 100.
- By the age of 80 it affects one person in five.

  Although the risk continues to rise, a majority of 90-year-olds are still unaffected.

A family condition
Some people are born at risk because of the genes they inherit.

Early onset
About 17,000 people in the UK are affected below the age of 65, sometimes as young as 35 years old. Alzheimer's disease in younger people often progresses more rapidly. A number of rare genetic faults make the disease more likely at a young age. Some people with a strong family history of Alzheimer's seek genetic counselling – to discuss whether they should have a test to see if they have inherited a faulty gene.

Late onset
A gene is also associated with Alzheimer's disease later in life. This is a variation of the apolipoprotein E gene (ApoE), which we all carry and which comes in three forms, ApoE2, 3 and 4. ApoE2 seems to protect against Alzheimer's, while ApoE4 seems to make it more likely. If we inherit one ApoE4 version we have an increased chance of the disease. If we inherit ApoE4 from both parents – as about two people in every 100 do – we are much more likely to develop the disease by the age of 80.

Brain damage

People who have had a severe head injury with loss of consciousness are at increased risk of dementia. This is also true of boxers who have become punch-drunk.

Down's syndrome

Because of their chromosomal defect, people with Down's syndrome are more likely to develop Alzheimer's disease. As more people with Down's syndrome survive into their 50s and 60s, more will develop the disease.

Other possible causes
- A possible association has been discovered with the cold sore virus, herpes simplex, but the link is complicated and seems also to include genetic factors.
- Some toxic chemicals put people at risk of Parkinson's disease. This has led to a search for a chemical link to Alzheimer's.
- There is no evidence of risk from aluminium saucepans or from drinking tea, which has traces of aluminium.

How is Alzheimer's disease diagnosed?

It is important not to become over-concerned at minor mental slips, but early and accurate diagnosis is important to clarify whether a treatable condition is causing symptoms, and to provide the best possible care.

A health professional records the pattern of symptoms, and uses simple tests to see what someone remembers and if they can hold simple information in the memory. These can be repeated after a few months to measure change. Where dementia is suspected brain scans can show chemical activity and whether areas of the brain are shrinking.

Diagnosis can be 80 to 90 per cent accurate in life but can only be confirmed after death.

Is treatment possible?

There is no cure for Alzheimer's disease and none is likely in the near future, but prospects for management have improved.

New drugs are being developed which seek to slow down the rate of mental decline. These are promising in the early stages of the disease, although it is unclear for how long they can help and they are not yet widely available. In April 1997, donepezil (Aricept) became the first drug to be licensed for Alzheimer's in Britain and other drugs such as rivastigmine (Exelon) are becoming available.

Affected people should live as normal a life for as long as they can. Memory aids and familiar routines are helpful. As the disease progresses, people need more support and may need close supervision and eventually nursing care.

© Alzheimer's Disease Society
October, 1998

Challenging dementia

10 key priorities for a new government . . .

1. The right to free health care
Action to re-emphasise the right of people to free health care as part of a long-term care system which is affordable, universal, equitable and open to all regardless of age.

2. National standards for community care
National standards for community care backed by adequate funding so that people with dementia and their carers have the same rights and can expect the same level of services wherever they live.

3. Training in dementia care for professionals
Training in dementia care for GPs and all health and social services professionals to ensure an effective and sensitive response to the needs of people with dementia and their carers.

4. Specialist services for younger people with dementia
Specialist local services for younger people with dementia and their carers which recognise their different life circumstances and needs.

5. The right to respite care
Legislation giving carers the right to respite care and enabling them to have a break from caring.

6. Improving financial support for carers
A review of carers' income, expenditure and benefits with a view to improving the financial support they receive.

7. Regulation of domiciliary care services
The introduction of regulation and inspection of domiciliary care services.

8. A legal framework for living wills
Legislation to establish a legal framework that will enable people to make decisions about their future care and treatment through living wills or a health care proxy.

9. Prevention of discrimination
Action to prevent insurers and employers from using genetic information to discriminate against people at risk of dementia in the future.

10. Greater funding of research
Greater government funding of research to step up the search for a cause and a cure for Alzheimer's disease and other forms of dementia.

Alzheimer's disease and other dementias
Some facts
- Alzheimer's disease is a physical illness which destroys the mind and memory. It is the most common form of dementia.
- There is no known cure, though new treatments are likely in the future which may help.
- Most of those with dementia are older people, but the disease can also strike individuals in their 30s, 40s and 50s.
- Dementia has devastating effects on both the person and those who care for them.
- Carers of people with dementia face a range of physical, emotional and financial difficulties.
- About one in four people with dementia lives alone in the community.

© Alzheimer's Disease Society

Living to be 100? It is nearly all in the mind

By David Fletcher, Health Correspondent

Taking regular exercise and keeping the mind active are the two essential ingredients in living to be 100 years of age, centenarians said yesterday.

A report based on interviews with 100 people who have passed their 100th birthday paints a picture of a good-humoured, independently-minded group, sometimes frustrated by difficulty in hearing or seeing but still interested in daily events.

One in four was still living alone and looking after themselves but two-thirds of those interviewed were living in nursing or care homes.

The report was compiled by the Distressed Gentlefolk's Aid Association, renamed Home, Residential and Nursing Care for Life, to mark its own 100th anniversary.

It said there are now more than 8,000 people over the age of 100 in Britain but predicts that on present trends their numbers will grow to 30,000 within 30 years.

By comparison, only 271 people were recorded as receiving telegrams from the Queen on their 100th birthday in 1952, the first year of her reign.

The report says many centenarians live in 'delightful' care homes, enjoying the companionship of others, and many commented on how helpful staff were to them.

'It has to be reported, however, that there were some examples of extremely poor care being given and some dreadful conditions in which residents were living.

'These included instances of staff paying no attention to residents, congregating together to chat and smoke, oblivious to the needs of residents.' The study found that most centenarians had a positive attitude to life with only four per cent expressing 'wholly negative' views.

> **A striking feature among many women centenarians – three-quarters of the total – was a strong streak of independence**

'They did not complain about difficulties they had encountered in the past and they were stoical about their present frailties.

'Several expressed their strong dislike of being frail and dependent but it was not a complaint just an expression of their frustration that, after a long and active life, they find themselves in such a position.'

A striking feature among many women centenarians – three-quarters of the total – was a strong streak of independence.

'This is partly demonstrated by their career patterns – the fact that many had experienced fulfilled working lives as a teacher, nurse, midwife, magistrate, shop assistant, photographer or needlewoman. Others had worked long over the age of retirement because they enjoyed working.'

The report found no single answer to the secret of long life. Eating good, natural food was frequently mentioned and living a moral life was cited by others. Being a teetotaller or non-smoker were not factors.

Three-quarters drank alcohol – some in the past and some continued to do so – and even more men reported smoking than drank alcohol.

In concludes: 'Those who have been, and have remained, intellectually active seemed to have the most positive outlook on life. It provided them with inner resources which could be called on when the frailty of the body took over.'

© Telegraph Group Limited, London 1997

ADDITIONAL RESOURCES

You might like to contact the following organisations for further information. Due to the increasing cost of postage, many organisations cannot respond to enquiries unless they receive a stamped, addressed envelope.

Action on Elder Abuse (AEA)
Astral House
1268 London Road
London, SW16 4ER
Tel: 0181 764 7648
Fax: 0181 679 4074
E-mail: aea@ace.org.uk
Action on Elder Abuse aims to prevent abuse in old age by raising awareness, encouraging education, promoting research and by collecting and disseminating information. It operates the Elder Abuse Response, a confidential helpline and information service, where you can obtain their catalogue *Working Together*, on freephone 0800 731 4141.

Age Concern England
Education Department
Astral House
London, SW16 4ER
Tel: 0181 679 8000
Fax: 0181 765 7211
E-mail: ace@ace.org.uk
Age Concern information line provides a service to older people, their relatives, friends, carers and professionals. To obtain written information on financial, legal issues, health, community care and housing issues, telephone Freephone 0800 009966 open 7 days a week, 7am to 7pm.

Alzheimer's Disease Society
Gordon House
10 Greencoat Place
London, SW1P 1PH
Tel: 0171 306 0606
Fax: 0171 306 0808
E-mail: info@alzheimers.org.uk
The Alzheimer's Disease Society produces a wide range of publications including, *What is Dementia*, a free factsheet, for anyone who is interested in dementia. They also have a helpline 0845 300 0336 (8am-6pm Monday to Friday) offering advice and support.

British Nutrition Foundation (BNF)
High Holborn House
52-54 High Holborn
London, WC1V 6RQ
Tel: 0171 404 6504
Fax: 0171 404 6747
E-mail: british/
nutrition@compuserve.com.
The (BNF) is an independent charity which provides reliable information and advice on nutrition and related health matters. They produce a wide range of leaflets, briefing papers and books. Ask for their publications list.

Centre for Policy on Ageing
25-31 Ironmongers Row
London, EC1V 3QP
Tel: 0171 253 1787
Fax: 0171 490 4206
E-mail: cpa@cpa.org.uk
An independent organisation which aims to raise issues of public importance on matters to do with ageing and old age.

Employers' Forum on Age
Astral House
1268 London Road
London, SW16 4ER
Tel: 0181 765 7280
Fax: 0181 765 7211
The Employers' Forum on Age is a network of leading employers who through first hand experience, know the business value of attracting and retaining experienced employees regardless of age.

Help the Aged
St James' Walk
London, EC1R 0BE
Tel: 0171 253 0253
Fax: 0171 250 4474
E-mail: info@helptheaged.org.uk
Aims to improve the quality of life for elderly people in the UK, particularly those who are frail, isolated or poor. Publishes useful factsheets and leaflets. They are unable to cope with large numbers of demands from students for the articles mentioned within this publication. They do however have other information which is available for research enquiries.

HelpAge International (HAI)
3rd Floor, 67-74 Saffron Hill
London, EC1N 8QX
Tel: 0171 404 7201
Fax: 0171 404 7203
E-mail: hai@helpage.org
HelpAge International is a global network of not-for-profit organisations working with and for disadvantaged older people worldwide to achieve a lasting improvement in the quality of their lives. There are over 50 member organisations throughout the world.

Research into Ageing
Baird House
15-17 St Cross Street
London, EC1N 8UW
Tel: 0171 404 6878
Fax: 0171 404 6816
E-mail: ria@ageing.co.uk
A registered charity which publishes a wide range of material aimed at those working with older people and for academics and students studying social policy, social work and social gerontology. However they are a small charity and are unable to respond to individual student requests. Teachers wanting copies of their leaflets will need to send an S.A.E. with their requests.

Royal College of Psychiatrists
17 Belgrave Square
London, SW1X 8PG
Tel: 0171 235 2351
Fax: 0171 235 1935
Produces an excellent series of free leaflets on various aspects of mental health. Supplied free of charge but a stamped, addressed envelope is required.

INDEX

abuse of elderly people 29, 32-3
age range of older people 1, 2, 3
ageing population
    in the UK 1
        and ageism in the workplace 15, 20, 21
        and world populations 2, 3, 9-10
ageing process 8-9
ageism in the workplace 15-24
    best practice guidelines 17
    call for legislation on 22
    costs of 19
    and industrial tribunals 18, 19
    and mixed age workforces 15, 16, 20
    reasons for 16
    and sex discrimination 17
    UK Code of Practice 15, 18, 20, 21
    and unemployment 15, 19, 23-4
Alzheimer's disease 35, 36-9
    causes 38-9
    diagnosis 36, 39
    early onset 38
    medication for 36, 39
    symptoms 38
arthritis 34

benefits (State)
    integrating tax and 32
    for pensioners 13-14
blindness 25
brain damage, and Alzheimer's disease 38

care for the elderly 26-33
    abuse and neglect 29, 32-3
    caring for each other 28
    costs of 26
    in developing countries 28-9
    and family break-ups 31-2
    finding a care home 26
    funding 27, 31
    at home 29
    information on care homes 29
    in NHS hospitals 30
    UN principles for 11
carers
    and dementia 36
    older people as 28, 29
    and respite care 36
    support for 29
    traditional 31
cataracts 25
cell ageing 8
centenarians, characteristics of 40

dementia 34, 35-9
    and carers 36
    common problems in 35-6

    in developing countries 10, 25
    government priorities on 39
    multi-infarct 35
    numbers affected by 35
    training in dementia care 39
    types of 35
    understanding and respecting people with 36-7
depression 34-5, 36
developing countries
    care of the elderly 28-9
    life expectancy 5, 9
    older people in 25
        and mental health problems 10, 25
        women 2, 4
    population ageing 2, 3, 9-10
discrimination
    and older women 4
    of people at risk of dementia 39
    and state pension age 1
    see also ageism in the workplace
diseases, age-related
    deaths from 10
    dementia 34, 35-9
    and depression 34
    genetic information on 5, 8-9
Down's syndrome, and Alzheimer's disease 38
drugs, for Alzheimer's disease 36, 39

economic activity
    and older people 16
        in developing countries 2, 4, 25, 28, 29
elder abuse 32-3
exercise, benefits of 9

families
    and care of the elderly 28, 31-2
    and the tax system 32

gender structure of the older population 1, 3, 4
genetics
    and age-related diseases 5, 8-9
    and Alzheimer's disease 38, 39

health
    genetic information on 5, 8-9
    and lifestyle 7, 9
healthy ageing 25
hospitals, care of the elderly in 30
households of retired people 1
human genome project 5

Income Support for pensioners 13
incontinence, and dementia 35

life expectancy
    in developing countries 5, 9

and mental health problems 34
in the UK 1, 5, 20
   regional variations in 7
in world populations 2, 3, 10
lifestyle, and health 7, 9
living wills 39

men
   life expectancy 1, 7
   pensionable age 1
mental health 34-9
   anxiety 34
   dementia 34, 35-9
   depression 34-5
   and elder abuse 33
   and population ageing 10, 25
   sleep problems 34

NHS (National Health Service), care of the elderly 30
nutrition 9

oldest old
   care of 28
   in the population 2, 3

Parkinson's disease 34, 35, 39

pensionable age 1
pensions 12-14
   occupational 14
   and 'redistribution' to the low-paid 12
   Serps (State Earnings Related Pension Scheme) 12, 13
   'stakeholder' second pensions 12
   State Retirement Pension 12, 13
population ageing *see* ageing population

redundancy
   age-based selection for 17
   coping with 23-4
respite care 36
rural areas, older people living in 3

self-employment, and older people 16
sleep problems 34, 35

taxation, integrating tax and benefits 32

unemployment, and workplace ageism 15, 19, 23-4
urban areas, older people living in 3

visual impairment 25

wealth, and older people 6

Independence Web News

[Back] [Forward] [Home]   [Reload] [Images] [Open] [Print] [Find]   [Stop]

[Live Home Page] [Search] [Computer] [Support] [System]

* * * * *

Age Concern England
http://www.ace.org.uk
Age Concern England's web site has factsheets covering the following subject areas: income, legal issues, health, community care and housing. The site provides details about their library service, statistics about older people, their publications, reading lists and a frequently asked questions (FAQs) section. Well worth a visit.

LinkAge 2000
http://library.advanced.org/10120/core.html
LinkAge 2000 is a web site created to provide students (ages 12-18) from around the world with the opportunity to interactively learn about ageing and older adults. In addition, LinkAge 2000 serves as a resource for teachers and educators who want to incorporate the study of ageing into the curriculum.

AgeInfo
http://www.unl.ac.uk:9999
AgeInfo is an information service about older people provided by the Library and Information Service of the Centre for Policy on Ageing. AgeInfo publishes a bibliographic database (AgeInfo), an organisations database (AgeOrgs) and a Calendar of Events database (Events).

Passport 50 Plus
http://www.passport50plus.org.uk/front.htm
Provides a vast amount of information and advice for the over-50s. Covers a wide range of issues including the following: health, family, home, work and retirement, money, travel and transport, goods and services, leisure, safety, the legal system and government.

The International Association of Gerontology
http://www.cas.flinders.edu.au/iag
Gerontology is the understanding, through scientific study, of the processes and the phenomena of ageing. This site is probably more relevant for further and higher education courses.

Administration on Ageing
http://www.AoA.DHHS.GOV/aoa/pages/info.html
Heavily US biased information but interesting. The site provide factsheets designed to help prepare people for the longevity revolution by heightening awareness to the demographics and challenges of the 21st Century. Each factsheet includes an overview of the subject and details related to Administration on Ageing initiatives. Also included are various resources listings that include federal agencies and national organisations as well as some suggested readings.

ACKNOWLEDGEMENTS

The publisher is grateful for permission to reproduce the following material.

While every care has been taken to trace and acknowledge copyright, the publisher tenders its apology for any accidental infringement or where copyright has proved untraceable. The publisher would be pleased to come to a suitable arrangement in any such case with the rightful owner.

Chapter One: The Older Population

The retired population, © Help the Aged, *Our ageing world – the facts*, © Helpage International, *World Population aged 60 and over, 1950-2050*, © United Nations Population Division, *The ageing of the world's population*, © United Nations/Division for Social Policy and Development, *Percentage of the world population aged 60 and over 1950-2150, medium fertility scenario*, © United Nations Population Division, *Older women*, © Helpage International, *UK lifespan 'is heading toward 80'*, © The Guardian, May 1998, *Age structure of deaths – worldwide*, © World Health Organisation (WHO), *You're never too young to be old*, First published in The Independent, September 1998, *A life in the South is 7 years longer*, © The Daily Mail, December, 1997, *The top . . . the bottom*, © The Daily Mail, December, 1997, *Ageing process*, © Research into Ageing, *Population ageing – a public health challenge*, © WHO/OMS, 1999, *Life expectancy at birth for both sexes*, © United Nations Population Division, *The UN principles for older persons*, © United Nations – Department of Public Information, New York, *Pensions timebomb*, © The Daily Mail, June 1998, *Current pension scheme membership by age and sex*, © Crown copyright is reproduced with the permission of the Controller of Her Majesty's Stationery Office, *Income*, © Help the Aged, *Pensioners' incomes*, © Crown copyright is reproduced with the permission of the Controller of Her Majesty's Stationery Office.

Chapter Two: Ageism in the Workplace

Age – the issues for today's workplace, © Employers' Forum on Age (EFA), *Age discrimination*, © Industrial Society, February 1999, *Age discrimination in job applications – 'too old'*, © Crown copyright is reproduced with the permission of the Controller of Her Majesty's Stationery Office, *Age prejudice 'costs Britain £26bn a year'*, © The Independent, November 1998, *The real cost of ageism*, © Employers' Forum on Age (EFA), *Ministers outlaw age limits on jobs*, © The Independent, August 1998, *Don't snub the golden oldies, bosses urged*, © The Daily Mail, August 1998, *Broken promises*, © The Guardian, November 1998, *Method of job search by age* © Crown copyright is reproduced with the permission of the Controller of Her Majesty's Stationery Office, *Private lives*, © The Guardian, November 1998.

Chapter Three: Health and Care Issues

Healthy ageing, © Helpage International, *Home truths*, © The Guardian, October 1998, *Town halls 'still plundering the elderly in care'*, © The Daily Mail, July 1998, *When older people need care . . .* , © Helpage International, *Old people's homes 'hide the true cost'*, © The Daily Mail, October 1998, *The 'invisible' patients*, © The Daily Mail, January 1999, *Family break-ups 'spell disaster for care of the elderly'*, © The Daily Mail, *Elder abuse*, © Action on Elder Abuse, *Mental illness*, © Crown copyright is reproduced with the permission of the Controller of Her Majesty's Stationery Office, *Statistics on dementia*, © Alzheimer's Disease Society, *Understanding and respecting the person with dementia*, © Alzheimer's Disease Society, October 1997, *What is Alzheimer's disease?*, © Alzheimer's Disease Society, October 1997, *Challenging dementia*, © Alzheimer's Disease Society, *Living to be 100? It is nearly all in the mind*, © Telegraph Group Limited, London 1997.

Photographs and illustrations:

Pages 1, 8, 11, 15, 16, 25, 31, 37: Simon Kneebone, pages 4, 13, 24, 28, 33: Pumpkin House, pages 18, 21, 27, 40: Ken Pyne.

Craig Donnellan
Cambridge
April, 1999